MW00339376

"Based on my 30 plus years of examining manage[...] for graduate-level courses, I think *Corporate Smoke[...]* format—fluent and easy to comprehend...hits all th[...] extremely helpful for systems thinking and team problem solving."

— M. Raymond Alvarez, DHA, FACHE, MPA

"I enjoyed it from cover to cover. As a seasoned issues management practitioner working with a wide range of industries, I recommend *Corporate Smokejumper* to senior executives who wonder if their companies are fully prepared for a major crisis. The book outlines a real-world approach to crisis management. The techniques have been tested and shown to be effective in today's fast-paced complex business environment."

— Kelly Henry, Owner, H&G Public Affairs, LLC

In a word, wonderful. If I could only have one reference source for effective crisis management, Gil Meyer's *Corporate Smokejumper* would be it. Meyer has compiled a wealth of experience and knowledge into a book that should be at the ready for a great many people. Wonderful real-life examples. A very readable format.

— Paul Dice, Executive Director, Millville, NJ Housing Authority

"As a veteran practitioner from the front-lines of crisis management who developed and ran his own business in this arena for 25 years, I can confirm that *Corporate Smokejumper* offers guidance that is enormously valuable to both the new professional in the field and the seasoned expert. The recommendations are vital for building and implementing an effective crisis management program."

— Ray Germann

"Gil was one of my first masters in the art of issues and crisis management. This book is an excellent way to learn firsthand the practical aspects of the art directly from one of the top global experts."

— Dr. Kiko Suarez

"I was fortunate to be in the field receiving support and guidance from Gil during my tenure as an Emergency Response leader for DuPont. Without the robust Crisis Management Program that Gil oversaw, success was not possible. His tools and techniques work. They are truly field-tested—I can attest. My experience shows that the program worked every time and in some very difficult situations. This program is a MUST HAVE."

— Tom Keefer, Special Programs and Development Manager, Specialized Professional Services, Inc.

Corporate Smokejumper by Gil Meyer, is a must-read for anyone responsible for public affairs, whether in the private, public or non-profit sector. It also is strongly recommended reading for CEOs and other senior managers. Mr. Meyer has written THE textbook on crisis preparedness, planning and management. Based on his frontline experience in navigating crises around the globe for multinational giant DuPont, he provides step-by-step guidelines for preparing for, responding to, and managing your way through a crisis. It is clear, concise and to-the-point with real-world scenarios seasoned with a dash of humor. When a crisis strikes, this is the book you need to have at your fingertips.

— Kevin Brown, Communications Executive

Corporate Smokejumper

Crisis Management:
Tools, Tales and
Techniques

by Gil Meyer

BLUE BLAZE BOOKS™

First Edition printing 2017

Published by Blue Blaze Books
Newark, DE 19711

Blueblazebooks.com
ISBN: 978-0-9913288-1-9

This book
is dedicated to:

Cyril "Nick" Meyer, my uncle and godfather,
a Pittsburgh firefighter who lost his life fighting a fire.
We owe firefighters a huge debt of gratitude.
Their quiet courage and dedication often goes unnoticed
until we, as individuals, need them.

Table of Contents

Preface

For more than 30 years I have been managing crises, and for more than 20 years I also have been teaching others how to be effective at crisis management. The information in this book is largely based on my real-world experience in crisis management at E. I. DuPont de Nemours and Company. Founded as a gunpowder mill on the banks of the Brandywine Creek near Wilmington, Delaware, in 1802, DuPont diversified over the next two hundred years and became a corporate conglomerate engaged in many commercial applications of science.

My crisis-management career experiences, however, began well before I joined DuPont in 1987. I knew when I was still in graduate school that I wanted a career in issue- and crisis-management. At that time, I worked for the West Virginia University Cooperative Extension Service's Pesticides and Chemicals office where I had my first opportunities to work on environmental controversies. After graduate school, I managed community relations at hazardous-waste sites for NUS Corporation, an environmental consulting firm, during the hottest days of the U.S. Environmental Protection Agency Superfund program. In the wake of Union Carbide's disaster in Bhopal, India, Bill Ruckelshaus, who was twice head of the U.S. EPA, set up a "bridging" organization to develop better ways to manage the interface between industry and its vocal critics. That pioneering organization was the National Institute for Chemical Studies, and I became its first Deputy Director.

When I began working at DuPont, the corporation had become

one of the largest chemical companies in the world. You probably have heard of DuPont, but if you were asked to list its products you might pause and then struggle to come up with more than a few. Some DuPont products you might know include Tyvek®, used to wrap new homes to make them more energy efficient, or Corian® or Zodiac® that you might have purchased for your kitchen counter. You might even know that the company made Kevlar®, the bullet-resistant material that protects soldiers and police officers—and even smokejumpers. Unless you are a firefighter, though, you probably don't know that the material protecting the bodies and lives of many in that band of heroes is Nomex®, another high-tech material made by DuPont.

No matter what your occupation, it's doubtful you are aware of the DuPont products in your smartphone, your flat-screen TV, your car, or your sporting goods. Nor would you likely know that DuPont's seed company, DuPont Pioneer, has been vital for many years in helping to feed the world. And unless you have been to Wilmington, Delaware, where the company's corporate headquarters have been located for more than 200 years, you might not know that DuPont also ran an elegant old-world-style hotel with two highly rated restaurants and a 1,200-seat playhouse for live theatre, meetings, and entertainment.

Because the crisis situations I discuss in this book relate to my real-world experiences at DuPont, I have changed some names and details, but the concepts are valid. I also draw on case studies outside DuPont. For the external case studies, I have been true to the facts as I understand them, but I know that relying on outside sources cannot give you a complete view of the real situation. Again, though, the concepts are valid.

In addition to colleagues with whom I worked inside these organizations, there also were instances where I worked with external consultants and lawyers. Likewise, I interacted with my crisis management counterparts in other companies and industry groups. In ways large and small, I learned from all of these professionals, many of whom are acknowledged at the end of this book.

There are innumerable factors that influence the outcome of any given crisis. I offer time-tested ideas for you to adopt or adapt and use as your judgment dictates. Also, audiences consistently tell me that "war stories" help them remember the vital lessons. In addition, they appreciate the wisdom imparted by quoting others. And they welcome some humor. By their very nature, crises are serious, but that does not mean we cannot have some laughs along the way. In fact, humor can be an important tool. Peppered throughout this book are war stories, quotations, and my own brand of humor.

Through the years I have collected the witless wisdom of people under stress. So as not to embarrass those individuals, I have created a fictitious business leader to voice all of the twisted thoughts, malapropisms, and downright dumb things I have heard. I also have made up some of the items myself to emphasize a point. Thus, I would like to introduce:

Stu Poore
Crisis Production Leader
Gudenuff Technology, LLC

Watch for some of Stu's witless crisis management "wisdom" throughout.

Finally, neither I nor DuPont nor any other party can be held liable for the outcome of your crisis, whether in whole or in part. Crisis management, by its very nature, is high risk and highly unpredictable.

Good companies do not just survive a crisis, they learn from it. The really good organizations even learn from near misses. They seek to capture lessons from problems that nearly became big crises. In the end, they and their crisis management teams come out the other side stronger, smarter, and better equipped to deal with the tumultuous world in which all companies do business.

—Gil Meyer
February 2017

CHAPTER

1

Already a Crisis?

If your company already is engulfed in a crisis, please go straight to Chapter 10.

But before you do, promise yourself that as soon as things calm down, you will come back to learn how to develop a more organized approach to crisis planning and preparedness.

Also, before you leap into the fire, know that you and your organization are likely to survive. Most crises do not destroy companies. They can, of course, inflict a great deal of damage to reputations and financial position. You will get through the challenges if you and your company maintain a firm ethical footing.

Now, take a deep breath and turn to Chapter 10.

CHAPTER

2

Crisis Management is a Journey

What's In This Chapter:

2.1 Congratulations on Making It This Far
2.2 What is a Smokejumper?
2.3 Managing Crises in a Complex Corporate Environment
2.4 You Likely Will Survive

2.1 Congratulations on Making It This Far

Congratulations on choosing to invest time and effort to get ready for a crisis! Far too many organizations assume either that their firm never will experience a crisis—despite the fact that the statistics say exactly the opposite—or, that if a crisis occurs, they can wing it and do just fine. You, on the other hand, are on your way to real crisis preparedness and competency.

> **Assuming you can create a crisis management program while you are in a crisis is like assuming you can install smoke detectors and a sprinkler system while your building is on fire.**

Be aware that crisis management in the corporate environment is a journey of constant improvement. There is no end to the journey. Each hour you invest makes you better prepared, but in the dynamic business world of today, crises come in so many shapes and flavors that there is no way any organization can declare itself fully prepared for absolutely anything that might happen.

It is entirely possible, however, to have a program for your company that allows you to be ready for key vulnerabilities relevant to *your* circumstances. In addition, it is entirely possible to have a program designed to anticipate the unexpected. This book will help you create a program that is flexible, scalable, and resilient so that you can respond efficiently and effectively to essentially any crisis that comes at you.

Key Points:

- ☑ Crisis Management is a journey. Get started, but know that you never will be done.

- ☑ Begin by tailoring your program to your specific vulnerabilities.

- ☑ Your program must be adaptable so that you can respond even to the unanticipated.

2.2 What is a Smokejumper?

Smokejumpers are a special type of firefighter. They parachute into remote areas to combat wildfires, hoping to reach a developing fire and extinguish it before it becomes a raging inferno consuming everything in its path. The highly disciplined men and women who battle wildland fires must carry their tools, gear, and supplies with them when they jump and then rely on their training, experience, judgment, and fitness to deal with threats and uncertainty, often in the harshest of conditions. The ordinary risk of a parachute jump, the adverse conditions for the jump, and the lack of additional resources for firefighting and rescue once on the ground in an isolated area give smokejumping a well-deserved reputation as exceedingly dangerous work.

There are, of course, some critical distinctions between the work of a smokejumper and the work of a corporate crisis manager, but there are certain similarities as well:

 ❋ Extreme personal risk. For a smokejumper, risks include stress, personal injury or even loss of life. For a corporate manager, the risks include stress, law suits, high-profile failure, personal reputation damage, demotion, or even loss of job and income.

✱ Both professions require individuals to jump into a volatile situation where the only thing they know for certain is that they will face a rapidly changing set of challenges where surprises are the norm.

✱ Both professionals enter the scene carrying a set of tools, and those tools are, by design, versatile and adaptable, especially given the training that smokejumpers undergo and the training a corporate crisis manager should have undergone.

✱ Perhaps most important is the experience each professional brings to the unfolding crisis.

The skills of a smokejumper have been sharpened like a finely honed ax blade and tested under extreme conditions. This book provides the corporate crisis manager with versatile tools and the training to begin using them. Like the smokejumper, however, to become proficient with the tools, a crisis manager must leap into real-world situations and put them to work. There is no substitute for being tested by fire.

2.3 Managing Crises in a Complex Corporate Environment

Almost 30 years of my crisis-management experience—including 12 years as global crisis management leader for DuPont—occurred in this widely diversified company with operations and sales all around the world. I sometimes learned that we were in a particular business only when my phone rang to tell me we had a problem. Figuratively, I often parachuted into a situation where I knew little about the terrain or the challenges I would face.

A study by Swiss Re, one of the largest reinsurance companies in the world, showed that natural and manmade disasters in 2015 resulted in losses of $92 billion.

Saying I was the global crisis manager for DuPont, understates the role, because in addition to having products on Earth, DuPont also has products on Mars. The planetary rovers—robotic vehicles that propel themselves around alien landscapes gathering and communicating data—exceeded all expectations for performance and longevity, and did so, in part, thanks to DuPont technology.

In this book, I repeatedly emphasize the importance of good stewardship and crisis prevention; however, not all crises are preventable. If nothing else, your business may be subject to devastation by uncontrollable forces of nature—severe storms or geologic upheavals—or by financial turmoil or political unrest. Furthermore, all businesses encounter people who simply make mistakes or use poor judgment. Bad things happen! You cannot prevent all of it.

2.4 You Will Likely Survive

Any company that lasts will experience at least one crisis situation. And those that don't last . . . well, that is a crisis of a different color. But with the planning you are doing and maybe with a little luck, odds are that you and your company will make it through the crises you face. That's the good news. The bad news is that crises can do much damage to an organization and to individuals. That is why this book is important: It is a survival guide that will help you get through a crisis and capture the valuable lessons of the experience as well.

CHAPTER

3

How Do I Know If a Problem Is Really a Crisis?

What's In This Chapter:

3.1 Formal Definition of a "Crisis"

The following definition of "crisis" was used in DuPont's formal Crisis Management Plan at the corporate level during my tenure at the company.

A crisis generally is an unexpected company-related event of a nature and magnitude that meets all of the following conditions:

* Adversely affects the normal operations, conduct of business, reputation, or financial position of the company

* Requires an immediate, coordinated management response

✱ Has the potential to quickly focus extensive media and public attention on the company

An important word in the definition is *all,* because the first two criteria could be met by a problem that does not constitute a corporate crisis. For example a serious supply-chain problem could involve the first two points. If a business cannot get key materials to make its products, that is somebody's crisis, but in most cases the situation does not rise to the level of a corporate crisis.

The third condition cited above is the one that moves the situation into the external spotlight and brings a new dimension to the problem. In the DuPont concept of crisis management, that outside attention was a critical factor.

 The Chinese write the word crisis as two characters: danger and opportunity. Thus, the symbol makes for a fitting description of what a crisis can mean to your company. Certainly there is danger, but in some cases there also can be opportunity... if managed correctly. One DuPont crisis greatly angered the company's customers whose businesses were adversely affected by a particular product-quality issue. Nonetheless, after the dust had settled and everything was resolved, a number of the customers complimented the company for how it handled the situation. In some regards, the company's reputation was enhanced and the bonds with customers strengthened.

3.2 Your Company's Definition of a Crisis

First, it is crucial for your organization to have an agreed-upon definition of a crisis. And second, people must understand which situations are "in scope" and should be managed under your crisis management program as well as which are "out of scope" and do not belong there.

 The crisis management program I led at DuPont was an "all risks" program. Any situation that met the formal definition of crisis stated above would be considered for handling within the scope of the company's crisis management structure. Other companies define the scope in different ways. Some are more operational or security focused, leaving areas such as financial crises to a different group.

Clearly defining what is in scope and out of scope may take some work. In fact, the criteria may emerge only over time when gray areas surface and you find your team debating whether the situation should be covered in the plan. In the event an urgent situation arises but there is uncertainty about whether it is in scope, you must, of course, ensure that it is managed effectively. You cannot waste time while the building is on fire debating who should hold the fire hose. Later you can debate whether it should or should not have been managed within your crisis system. Toward the end of the book, there is guidance on conducting a debrief to assess how things went. One topic to discuss in the debrief can be whether the "urgent" problem was within the intended scope of your crisis plan. The next question is whether it should be in scope even if it was not already. You own the plan—adapt it to your needs.

> **Your Crisis Management Plan must have a formal definition.**
>
> **All involved people must be clear on what is in scope and out of scope. Senior leaders and the crisis team itself must all be in agreement concerning what is covered by your plan and what is not.**

....

"Two men in a burning house must not stop to argue."
—African proverb

....

As you get started, take a best guess on what should be in scope for your crisis management program. Base the guess on the Vulnerability Assessment you conduct. (See Chapter 7, Section 2.)

3.3 A Shorthand Definition

Over the years I came to realize that although a formal definition of "crisis" is needed, there is an informal definition that carries important insights. In the final analysis, a crisis is a high-profile, high-stakes situation where you are faced with a range of bad choices and no time to develop new ones. Moreover, you often must address the situation in the glare of the public spotlight.

Etymology of the word Crisis:

From the Ancient Greek—krisis— meaning decision, choice, election, judgment, dispute.

After all, if there were an obvious good choice, the business would embrace it, and there would not be a crisis. Many times my phone at DuPont would ring, and the caller would say, "I'm the manager of one of the businesses. We have a really bad situation, and we don't know what to do."

Never once in all my years leading crisis management did I get a call from someone who said, "We have a really big problem, and we know how to fix it." I never was invited to the meetings where there was a good way to fix a problem and everyone agreed to it. I was invited only when the group got stuck.

Key Point:

☑ A crisis is a high-profile, high-stakes situation where you are faced with a range of bad choices. Nonetheless, you must make a choice and move forward. You must make high-stakes decisions with too little information—or with faulty information. You have very little time, yet you must move into the public spotlight where everyone will second-guess what you decide to do. From that point on, you will live with the consequences of your move.

A particularly irksome aspect of making a crisis decision is that once in the spotlight, it frequently will look like it was a really bad choice. That's because it was. Remember, you had only bad choices. If you want to see what this second-guessing looks like, watch the movie *Sully*. After successfully landing a plane full of people on the Hudson River, the plane's captain is relentlessly grilled by the National Transportation Safety Board for making the wrong decision. So when someone says, "That was a bad move," he or she could be right. The problem is that they likely never will be privy to the other options. All they can see is how poor this one looks. In Chapter 14, Section 3, there is a decision-making tool that guides the sorting and selection process. It may not totally solve the dilemma, but it definitely will help the team choose from what is often a bewildering array of bad options.

People who get involved with crisis management must have a thick skin. They need to be able to deal with criticism even when there is no opportunity for self-defense, because highlighting the inner workings of the team might compromise the situation.

"Making a crisis decision is like hitting a golf ball in a concrete room. You can tee it up and try to aim all you want, but there is a reasonable probability it will come back and strike you in the head."
—Stu Poore, Crisis Production Leader, Gudenuff Technology

Ironically, at the same time the same crisis management professionals need a thick skin, they also have to be sensitive. To guide a crisis team effectively, the leader must be aware of not only what people are thinking and saying but also what they are feeling and what they are afraid to say.

3.4 An "Issue" or a "Crisis?"

Periodically, I am asked: What is the difference between an issue and a crisis?

The earlier discussion of what constitutes a "crisis" can be contrasted with the definition of "issue." An issue is an internal or external condition that must be met with an orderly response before it can have a significant adverse effect on the functioning and future interests of the company.

An issue, then, is an ongoing condition— or, at least, an emerging situation— that must be managed before becoming a crisis, whereas a crisis

An "Issue" is a protracted situation.

A "Crisis" is an acute situation.

Effective Issues Management can help in crisis prevention.

Centering Issues Management and Crisis Management in one part of the organization creates synergies.

is a more acute and focused circumstance, often with immediate and particular decision points. In practice, an issue can spike into a crisis or a crisis can flatten into an issue with which the company may have to deal for some time to come. Of course, a crisis can last for a long time as well. It is not uncommon for there to be a natural blurring of the lines between the terms issue and crisis.

 "I don't like to call things a crisis because it makes me look bad. If I call them an issue, then I look smarter."
—Stu Poore, Crisis Production Leader, Gudenuff Technology

In reality, the distinctions largely can be set aside. I never found a great deal of value in debating whether a problem was an issue or a crisis. My attitude always has been: If it's a significant problem, then manage it. Many of the tools and techniques you use are the same.

3.5 The Connection of Stewardship to Issue Management and Crisis Management

Your company's crisis management program should be like your community's fire brigade. You want to know that your town has first-rate firefighters but you don't want them racing to your house frequently. Similarly, you want your company to have a robust crisis management program, but you don't want to have to use it frequently. If your organization habitually has crises, you need to examine your stewardship efforts.

As Smokey Bear tells us: When it comes to forest fires, the primary goal is prevention. Likewise, your first goal in crisis management is crisis prevention. The inverted triangle depicts the relationship between stewardship, issues management, and crisis management.

Stewardship

Issues Management

Crisis Mgmt

Good stewardship consists of carefully and responsibly assessing and meeting the needs and expectations of customers, shareholders, employees and society at large. Because good stewardship pays in two ways, smart businesses invest in good stewardship.

Stakeholders can include:

* Society
* Customers
* Shareholders
* Employees

> **Definition of Stewardship:**
> Anticipating and addressing the needs and expectations of key stakeholders in a responsible and timely manner.

3.6 Stewardship Pays Once

The first way stewardship investments pay off is by directly preventing crises. Good care of your business and doing what is right in the eyes of your stakeholders will go a long way toward preventing crises. At DuPont, alignment with stakeholder expectations always began with adhering to the company's Core Values.

Key Point:

☑ DuPont Core Values
- Highest Ethics
- Respect for People
- Safety and Health
- Environmental Stewardship

Most companies have stated core values. It is crucial that they are more than just words on a page; they must be indisputable concepts that guide the organization. If they are only words that no one attends to, they are like a railing not bolted to a balcony. When you lean on the railing, it will fail you. Similarly, if your core values are not tied to how the business operates, you will be in a worse position than if you never had believed in the first place that something was there to sustain you.

Chapter 6 goes into more detail about how to make your core values shine brightly on the dark days of a crisis. For now, the key point is that they can and should guide your stewardship efforts.

Issues often arise when there are gaps between stakeholder expectations and the company's behavior. An issue can serve as a smoke detector that alerts you to a problem before it grows into a crisis and your company ends up fully engulfed in flames. An issue that is not well managed can spike into a crisis if not dealt with when the situation is still manageable.

 "My company has one Core Value. It is: 'Try to obey the law.' We think that is enough of a stretch for the way we operate."
—Stu Poore, Crisis Production Leader, Gudenuff Technology

As an example: If the community surrounding one of your facilities believes you should operate in a certain way—perhaps in relation to noise or truck traffic—and the perception is that you are falling short, you have an issue to manage.

If the excessive noise from your facility is not effectively managed, the issue is not likely to go away on its own. One morning, your employees may arrive at work only to find members of a community group chained to the gate and blocking the entry. The group is already posting about the protest on social media, and they have invited the news media to the site of the protest to make their grievances publicly known. Now you have a crisis to manage.

> If your Core Values are just words on a page, they are like a railing not bolted to a balcony. When you need the railing, it will fail you.

Had your stewardship program attended to the community's concerns, you could have dealt with the issue and prevented the crisis. Relations with the community would have remained cordial, and your operation would have gone on with business-as-usual rather than having experienced a disruption.

Key Point:

☑ Good stewardship pays by preventing both issues and crises

Good stewardship pays in preventing problems. Most often good stewardship takes the form of running a quality operation that produces great products or services in a manner that is acceptable to the community at large.

3.7 Stewardship Pays Twice

Good stewardship also can pay dividends even if a crisis does occur. Imagine you have a good quality-control program for your products to make sure they perform as intended for your customers. One day you start getting calls that your products are not performing properly. Quickly the problem makes its way into the pages of the newspaper and is getting a lot of negative buzz through social media. Your reputation, profitability, and market share are at risk.

The first thing you point to when you begin to analyze the problem will be your solid quality-control program. As quickly as you can, you will assess what happened that allowed defective products to be made or delivered—if in fact they were defective. And you will tell customers, the news media, and other interested parties: "We have a program designed to prevent this sort of problem. If defective products did make it into the marketplace, clearly something has gone wrong. This is not how we do business. We will find the problem and fix it."

When you frame the problem as an anomaly, an outlier, chances are good that you will be believed. When asked for the details of your quality controls, you will relate them. Moreover, you will have a basis for locating the problem and correcting it. Thus, stewardship pays again as it protects your reputation and narrows the scope of analysis of the situation both within the company and by those on the outside.

3.8 A Clear Window and an Open Door

A rising expectation of many stakeholders is transparency. Especially when people perceive that the matters of concern may impinge on their interests, they believe they should have full and unfettered access to information.

Such a demand can create daunting challenges for a company already stretched by a crisis. The material being requested may include data that are incomplete or not yet interpreted. The information also could be misunderstood because it is out of context or is so technical the average person cannot accurately assess what is being shared. In addition, the information may be voluminous and a burden to assemble. Other concerns can include confidentiality and intellectual property value.

When people ask to see the data and the reports to substantiate what you are saying, many times they are telling you they do not trust the communications from your company. When you say something is safe, they say, "Prove it."

"Trust" is a simple word but a complex concept. Much of what happens during a crisis revolves around whether stakeholders believe they can trust you. In fact, trust is the central element of successful crisis management.

The need for trust begins within the crisis team itself, extends throughout your organization, and quickly moves to encompass all key external parties engaged in the situation.

Key Point:

☑ Trust is the central element of successful crisis management.

 WAR STORY | **Tell and Show**

When DuPont was working with a local community regarding the company's intention to build a hazardous waste incinerator at a large manufacturing facility in the U.S., nearby neighbors voiced concerns about emissions from the incinerator's stack that could include dioxins, a notorious class of compounds, some of which can be toxic.

DuPont told the neighbors that it was using the most advanced technology and that the emissions easily would fall within EPA specifications for safety.

"How will we know if you miss?" they asked.

"We'll give you a report at the end of each month."

"But if you missed during the month, then our kids already will have been exposed."

Because this incident was pre-internet, our response was to set up a monitoring station at the local library where people could go to look at real-time emissions data. It's doubtful that many of the concerned parents ever did, but the effort was decidedly worthwhile. It signaled our willingness to listen, to respond, and to be transparent.

With the Internet, it is easier than ever to provide information. The ability to give quick access to facts and figures can be good, but the possibility of immediate access also engenders higher expectations for even greater openness.

CHAPTER

4

The Fire Alarm

What's In This Chapter:

4.1   How Much Warning?
4.2   Ignoring the Fire Alarm

4.1 How Much Warning?

How much advance warning you will get when a crisis strikes varies widely. Some situations provide little or none, while others "phone ahead" to tell you to get ready.

> ❋ **Long lead time**— Some crises offer long periods during which you know the train is coming, although you may not know the exact arrival time. In certain situations you have years to prepare. For instance, new government regulations that will significantly change a company's ability to operate often are rife with delays. Failure to heed the warning and prepare for action in the months or even years before implementation creates a crisis. Other situations are not so clear. A new government safety study, for example, might contain unknowns for the business even though a report clearly is being prepared. In that case, it is still possible to prepare for a range of scenarios.

> ❋ **Short lead time**— With some crises, a hurricane, for example, the advance warning period is relatively short. Although the weather forecast regarding its strength and

path may be somewhat imprecise, a hurricane is a known threat days in advance. Ideally, before the storm or any crisis occurs, you will have conducted a vulnerability assessment (detailed in Chapter 7) to identify potential threats to your assets and to lay out a plan, in this case to deal with a storm and its aftermath. A vulnerability assessment can provide you a measure of preparedness. It will have alerted you to the complexity of the impending situation, and thus you will have thought through various actions your company might need to take. You then can make good use of the short lead time to deal with the specifics. The same is true for a wide range of potential crises beyond weather-related problems.

* No lead time— Many types of crises arise seemingly out of nowhere. An earthquake happens suddenly. If you have operations in known earthquake zones, you try to be as prepared as possible. Nonetheless, the devastation can be abrupt and severe.

* You pull the trigger— Perhaps the most gut-wrenching situation is when your company discovers a problem that is unknown to its outside stakeholders. The internal angst is enormous while company leaders wrestle with whether and how to notify customers, government officials, and others about the predicament.

Countdown to a Crisis

Hurricanes and typhoons are almost always anticipated many days in advance. Unfortunately, the state of forecasting technology still does not provide great precision on the storm system. At DuPont, we developed a 5-4-3-2-1 crisis countdown system for an approaching storm to balance any uncertainties with efforts to prepare. Let's say, for example, the company has facilities in the projection cone for the path of a hurricane. As noted, even advanced forecasting technology does not provide specific information on the path or strength of a storm system. What do we do?

* 5 days out, teams begin some basic efforts to prepare.

* 4 days out, if facilities remain in the cone, the intensity of preparation increases.

✱ 3 days out, if a significant storm still threatens, teams are in full swing implementing plans that already exist for every site in the area, and the company's emergency response teams are mobilizing from outside the storm zone so they can be staged at a location out of reach of the severe impact area but close enough so trucks carrying all the resources that may be needed can be driven through the tail end of the storm.

✱ 2 days out, final arrangements are being made.

✱ 1 day before landfall, all preparations are complete and teams are organizing the initial communications and actions that will occur as soon as the storm passes and damage assessments can begin.

How much warning? Some examples:

✱ **Uncertain timing**— The government is slated to issue a report that will be disruptive to your company's ability to do business, but timing for implementation of any mandates is uncertain. In one case, I watched governmental delays go on for years. We could hear the clock ticking but didn't know what time it was. Sitting under the Sword of Damocles for an extended period creates its own set of challenges.

✱ **Less than a day**—Periodically, a company will have limited advance notice that a problem is about to erupt. Sometimes you have a few hours to prepare. For example, a reporter calls and asks, "After Greenpeace holds its news conference tomorrow announcing that your company has done x, y, and z, will you have a spokesperson available to comment?" Other times news, or even rumors, rapidly transmitted via social media can act as a smoke detector that alerts you to imminent action against your company, giving you a brief period of time to put a plan into action.

✱ **None**—A tornado strikes a key facility. Disaster is upon you, and you have essentially no time to react. Only your early preparedness efforts will come into play as you immediately begin to deal with the calamity.

✱ **You pull the trigger**—Sometimes you must decide when to announce a previously unknown problem. As an example, in early 2012, the Coca-Cola Company learned that some orange trees in Brazil had been sprayed with an unapproved fungicide. When testing proved the fungicide was in one of the Coca-Cola orange juice products, the company notified federal regulators in the U.S., knowing the news would create concerns. Nonetheless, Coca-Cola's action put the company on the same side as the authorities and allowed it to move through the situation in a forthright manner.

WAR STORY | Front Lines of Greenpeace Protests

When DuPont announced a phase-out of chlorofluorocarbons because of their potential to damage the ozone layer, prominent environmental organization Greenpeace created a campaign to push for an immediate stop to production of CFCs (widely used in refrigerants, aerosol propellants, and other materials). DuPont knew this move would be highly disruptive to many systems such as those that provide refrigeration for food and medicine. Nonetheless, Greenpeace persisted in launching various attacks against the company's production sites.

DuPont had just navigated one round of protests when we got word one morning that another protest was being planned and would occur in about two weeks at a large DuPont production facility in New Jersey, directly across the Delaware River from corporate headquarters. That advance warning was most welcome, because previously we had been caught by surprise.

We assembled with our boss to get ready. I was part of the three-person SWAT team that routinely dealt with protests. The boss closed his office door and said defiantly, "This time we will be ready!"

We'd been discussing our plans for about 20 minutes when a coworker stuck her head in the room. When chastised by the boss, who said we were not to be interrupted because of the crucial work that had to be done, the intruder said that what she had to say could not wait. The boss retorted that we were planning for a soon-to-come Greenpeace protest and were not to be bothered. Smirking, she said, "Well, excuse me, but I thought you would be interested to know that Greenpeace activists are already on the water tower at the plant and are unfurling a large banner people can see as they cross the bridge."

She was correct. Greenpeace "commandos" had come ashore in New Jersey in Zodiac rafts at night and had made their way through the plant, then scaled the water tower adjacent to the huge, double-span Delaware Memorial Bridge, a primary

East Coast artery for people heading to New York City.

Chagrined, our boss jumped to his feet and yelled at his SWAT team: "Well, get going! You guys have been through this before. You know what to do. Get your stuff and get over to the plant."

He was right—we had been through this before. However none of us knew that a comedy of errors was just beginning.

My two colleagues and I agreed we would meet by the elevator in five minutes and raced off to gather up our materials and other gear. When we assembled in the lobby, coworkers wished us well as we zoomed off to deal with a hot and hostile situation. On the way down in the elevator, I commented that I had no car because I had ridden a bus to work. My SWAT-team companions said they, too, had taken a bus. Before we reached the ground floor, we realized we had no way to get across the river. So we pushed the button to go back to the 13th floor.

When the teammates who had cheered us as we departed saw us return and heard why, the cheers turned to jeers. One asked why we couldn't just swim over. Another suggested that Greenpeace might let us borrow one of the empty Zodiac rafts on the opposite riverbank. Eventually, one kind soul loaned us a car, and we were soon on our way again.

When we arrived at the main gate of the plant in New Jersey, news reporters and cameramen already were waiting. Once inside, we quickly decided my SWAT-team colleagues should accompany the plant manager to the gate to provide a statement to the press while I stayed in a conference room to start fielding the barrage of media calls coming in.

When hanging up from one call, I saw a DuPont security guard standing in the doorway. He said the leader of the Greenpeace team had asked if we would be willing to meet with him. Specifically, he wanted to talk with the plant manager. Seeing this opportunity to talk as a possible way to wind down the situation, I said sure.

A little while later, the security guard was back at the door. He said, "Well?"

"Well . . . what?" I replied,

"Okay," he said.

"Okay, what?"

"He's there."

"Who's where?" I asked.

"The leader of Greenpeace. He's in the plant manager's office."

"With whom?"

"Nobody. The plant manager is still out at the gate."

I jumped up and said, "You get down to that office and do not leave him alone for one second!"

As it turned out, the last laughs were on Greenpeace. The banner they unfurled was in the form of a huge blue ribbon that faced the bridge. Unfortunately for them, thanks to the winds rippling the material and the small size of the print, nobody could read the banner from the bridge, so they simply assumed DuPont had received some sort of big award.

Adding insult to injury, in a sidebar article to other coverage of the situation, the Wilmington News Journal ran a story on all of the DuPont products Greenpeace was using in its efforts to protest DuPont chemical compounds. It had to diminish some of the righteous indignation in the Greenpeace messages when it was noted that among the many products they were using, their coolers contained foam made with the reviled CFCs.

Finally, in order to avoid endangering anyone in trying to get the people off the water tower, we decided to let them stay there as long as they wanted. After three days, they announced they were coming down. Characteristically, they had media assembled at the main gate for their triumphant exit, which they knew would be in a police van because they were to be charged with trespassing. What they did not consider was that there was more than one gate at the plant, and the police van took an alternate route. While the media remained waiting at the plant's main gate, the Greenpeace folks already had been whisked away and booked at the police station.

4.2 Ignoring the Fire Alarm

Although crises often seem to fall suddenly from the sky, in fact, most often there are warning signals that are ignored or missed entirely. Some of the major disasters of our day not only were predictable, they actually had been foretold.

September 11, 2001— The World Trade Center in New York City was bombed in 1993, leaving six dead and thousands injured. Certain the WTC would be attacked a second time, Rick Rescorla, Security Director for Morgan Stanley, drilled and drilled on what the Morgan Stanley people were to do should there be another assault. His preparations saved many lives on the fateful day, eight years later, when the twin towers were completely destroyed and thousands were injured or killed. Sadly, Mr. Rescorla's approach was unique.

Hurricane Katrina— The powerful storm that devastated New Orleans and the Gulf Coast in August 2005 matched, in eerie detail, a story published by National Geographic in 2004 about what might happen if a major hurricane were to strike the New Orleans area. National Public Radio reported that the New Orleans Times-Picayune separately had predicted the devastation as well.

Financial Crisis of 2008— Multiple economists publicly predicted in large measure what happened in 2008. Ben Bernanke, former chairman of the Federal Reserve, after-the-fact stated in a *Forbes Magazine* article dated August 27, 2014, that the financial crisis of 2008 was the worst "in global history, including the Great Depression."

Superstorm Sandy— People were stunned by the devastation wrought by Superstorm Sandy in 2012. In the 1970s, however, laws had been passed requiring organizations to prepare for just such a storm. Experts believed it could happen and tried to get people to be ready. Few heeded the warning.

....

> *"One of the tests of leadership is the ability to recognize a problem before it becomes an emergency."*
> —*Arnold H. Glasgow, Author and Humorist*

....

Large and small, disasters are largely foreseeable. Warnings are sounded but typically are ignored. Questions arise:

* Why do we so often ignore the warnings?

* What can we do to sort the relevant threats from the cacophony of noise?

* What can we do about the heedlessness, lack of interest, and outright denial?

- Can we, in our small spheres, do something to prepare for a crisis in order to prevent or mitigate the damage to our own lives and companies?

- Can we change the behavior of others?

Why Do We Ignore the Alarms?

There are many reasons why we ignore the warnings.

✱ The most obvious answer is that there are too many warnings, alarms, buzzers, and clanging bells. If we were moved to action every time someone warned of an impending disaster, we would have time for nothing else. Alarms are far too common and most often are meaningless. Note what you do the next time you hear a car alarm in a parking lot. In all likelihood, you will do nothing in response.

✱ A second answer is inertia. There are vested interests that defend—actively or passively—the status quo. Observe how people rebuild in the same place after a hurricane and fight against protective measures such as sand dunes.

✱ Responding to warnings requires resources.

✱ Planning for possible disasters is not a priority, and, worse, is more often seen as a distraction. One can only imagine the griping that must have occurred at Morgan Stanley's offices in the WTC when Mr. Rescorla made the employees practice escaping.

To add to the difficulty, those who urge others to respond to warnings can be perceived as either:

a. Chicken Little, who misread signals and created unwarranted alarm, or

b. The Boy Who Cried Wolf. Lest the lesson be missed here, recall that the wolf actually came, but by then no one was listening to the warnings.

What can we do?

Since people have a proven tendency to go around with their fingers in their ears when alarms are sounding, what can we do?

We can start by sorting risks based on impacts and probabilities and also by factoring in our ability to reduce our vulnerability to threats. Begin by examining how your company is scanning for risks.

✱ Who is scanning?

✱ How is that information assessed?

✱ What happens regarding the lessons from near-miss crises?

This assessment should not be, and generally is not, a separate endeavor from the rest of how we operate our businesses and spend our lives. We constantly assess and address risks. They usually tend to be the micro risks that have the potential to impact our lives. Crossing a busy street is a common example.

⚠ *Pitfall – Confusing uncertain timing with uncertainty about the probability that something will actually occur.*

CASE STUDY | **The Rise in Oil Prices**

Long before the extreme spike in the price of oil in 2008, experts warned, with a high degree of certainty that the price would rise markedly at some point. Only the timing was unknown.

What might you do with advance information that the price of oil would increase, even if you did not know exactly when? It takes some effort, but not too much, to incorporate a rise in oil prices in your decision-making and then analyze what that scenario would mean relative to decisions made in the calm before that storm.

For example, if you were looking to buy a house in 2006 when oil was $60 a barrel, you could simply ask: "If we buy a big house far out in the country and the price of energy goes way up, how would that impact us?"

It doesn't take any research to know that it would be more expensive to heat and cool the big house; it would cost more to commute; and the property value could drop since demand for such homes would be lower due to the greater costs for heating and cooling and for the expensive commute.

But that's not the end of the discussion. Knowing it will cost more for power, light, and transportation doesn't mean you can't buy the house; it's just one consideration. A lower crime rate in the country may make you decide that this option is better than living in the city. The point is to stop to think about it. Then, if you buy the house and the price of oil spikes to $140 a barrel, at least you have considered that scenario.

⚠ *Pitfall – Assuming that since you cannot do anything to stop a mega-problem, you cannot do anything to mitigate the impact on yourself, your family, or your company.*

CASE STUDY | The Financial Crisis

In the years of rapidly increasing property values leading up to 2008, lots of folks believed the sub-prime mortgage lending practices of some banks made no sense or even were unethical. Some people went so far as to warn that approving large loans to people who likely would not be able to repay them was a recipe for disaster. Most people, though, thought there was nothing they could do to prevent such dealings.

There are two parts to that thought process, however, and many people get stuck on the first part. It is true that individual citizens are not going to get the banks and regulators and government programs to shift from such practices. That does not mean, though, that those same individuals cannot do anything to prevent the impact of a given disaster from pulling them under.

First, do not assume that a deal, a situation, or a policy is good, acceptable, or legal because someone else says it is. Stop to think about why an employee of a company with a questionable policy (for example, the person trying to sell you a mortgage) might want the public to perceive that policy as sound.

Use common sense. If it doesn't seem right that you could afford that much house on your income, ask detailed questions of people who don't have a vested interest in saying "everything's okay."

⚠ *Pitfall – Assuming that history is always a good predictor of the future.*

Don't assume the only future scenario is an extension of the current situation. "Home values have gone up by double digits annually around here for 10 years. Don't you want to get in on that?" A historic pattern is not the only information to consider.

CASE STUDY | Driving to Work

One of the greatest risks you face relative to both probability and impact is driving a motor vehicle. Most Americans drive on a daily basis. Clearly, they are well aware of the risks because they listen to traffic reports while they are driving, and those reports tell them, in real time, that the risks are irrefutable. "We have an accident with injuries on the interstate..." Moreover, on a fairly regular basis, they see the accidents firsthand or they know people who have been injured or have died in auto accidents. Just because you have not been in a wreck does not mean you won't be.

⚠ *Pitfall – Considering only the easiest, the most obvious, or the most desirable options.*

CASE STUDY | The World Trade Center, New York City

Imagine that it is early 2001. You have a high-paying job with a good company in New York City. Your office is in the World Trade Center. But your gut instinct tells you that working in the WTC is risky because it was a terrorist target some seven years earlier. What options might you consider? You are highly likely to begin discounting most of those options quickly because the easiest and most desirable choice—based on the belief that thousands of smart people are content to work in the twin towers—is that it must be reasonably safe to remain there.

The first step for avoiding these pitfalls is awareness. Be alert that these errors in thinking are common. The next step is to ask: What if? What if the future does not emerge the way your assumptions have planned for it? Finally, make space in your process for creativity and alternative ways to approach the problem. Working to avoid the pitfalls does not need to take a great deal of time, but it can pay huge dividends.

CHAPTER

5

Anatomy of a Crisis

What's In This Chapter:

5.1 How a Crisis Emerges

There are patterns to how a typical crisis develops. In many cases, there are initial warning signals that are ignored, discounted, or underestimated. Then a triggering event occurs. Sometimes there are also compounding events that make an initial circumstance worse than it otherwise would have been. Superstorm Sandy in 2012 is a good example of circumstances stacking up to create disaster. Sandy was barely a hurricane when it approached the coast of New Jersey, yet other weather conditions combined with it to create a "perfect storm" that left more than 50 people dead, many thousands of homes and vehicles destroyed, and more than $30 billion in total damages.

Whether or not there were warning signals, when a crisis progresses, external parties begin to gain an awareness of your critical situation. There may be a news article, some social media buzz, perhaps a government report. The problem also, quite literally, could erupt into an explosion.

The sequence of events in the development of a crisis has changed since I first started tracking these patterns many years ago. Originally, the factors related to litigation and class action lawsuits often had a lag time from the inception of the crisis. Now, particularly in the U.S., lawyers are present almost immediately in most crisis situations.

Key Point:

☑ Try this to see how quickly lawyers enter the scene of a crisis today: the next time you see "breaking news" about an industrial accident or major product recall, Google the topic. At the top of the search results, you will see paid advertisements for attorneys who wish to represent possible victims. In one warehouse fire that involved some DuPont products, three class-action lawsuits were filed while the smoke was still rising from the fire.

The lawyers on your team will play a crucial role in helping your team respond to a crisis. From the very beginning, especially in the U.S., you must be thinking about the litigation that frequently comes with a crisis. There are actions you must take at the outset to properly prepare for the lawsuits that will come. If litigation gets traction, you will be dealing with it for many years.

Depending on your ability to address the public's interest in the crisis, there can be discussion in traditional or social media that continues for weeks, months or even years. In addition, special interest groups may latch onto your crisis and leverage it for their own objectives, often citing your crisis as an example of why the changes they espouse are needed.

A crisis that carries fervent interest sustained over time becomes an added problem in that journalists will be competing for new angles on the story. They will look more broadly at your overall corporate behavior and more deeply into what actually happened in the particular situation. Often these investigative reporters will find enough material to propel the story forward news cycle after news cycle.

With sufficient public outcry, politicians will get involved. There will be comments and direct contacts from elected officials, followed by government hearings. Some crises leave a legacy of new laws and regulations intended to prevent the same type of problem from happening again.

Eventually, business schools and others may use your situation as a case study so that people will fully understand all that went wrong. Such analysis will be published in journals and on the Internet, making the information readily available for citation in perpetuity.

For a select few events, there is the ultimate status of becoming a crisis icon. Three Mile Island, Bhopal, Exxon Valdez, Deepwater Horizon, Chernobyl, Titanic, and Fukushima are examples of disasters that loomed so large in scope and in the news that even decades later from the name alone people instantly conjure up images of tragic loss or of terrifying threats to humanity, to other living creatures, and to the environment.

5.2 Jumping Through a Narrow Window

Not so many years ago, crisis management experts talked of the "golden hours of crisis response"—the five hours or so in which a company could position itself to respond when first facing a crisis. Now, with instantaneous coverage through digital technology and social media, that golden time has shrunk to five minutes, if you're lucky—less in many cases. In some circumstances, by the time you learn of the crisis, you already are behind.

For all practical purposes, a crisis manager must hit the ground running as soon as the crisis erupts. In later chapters, there are specific tools and techniques that will ensure you are always prepared to jump into your running shoes. The dynamics and demands of instant crisis response underscore the mandate to have a highly-efficient alert system, a well-trained team at the ready, and some well-honed techniques for rapid response.

"We haven't the time to take our time."

—Eugene Ionesco

The narrow window for response also underscores the need to pay attention to the warning signals. While you must avoid the temptation to sound the alarm for every possible concern, you should be actively investigating whether there is a smoldering ember that could trigger a conflagration.

 "Our crisis manager can't tell the difference between a Bic lighter and a flamethrower."

—Stu Poore, Crisis Production Leader, Gudenuff Technology

5.3 Three Groupings: On-site, Off-site, Business/Corporate

When you conduct your Vulnerability Assessment, it is easy to become overwhelmed by the wide array of crises that might befall your organization, including natural disasters, workplace violence, disease, kidnappings, embezzlement, cyber attacks, death of the CEO, and product recalls. While you will want to prepare in detail for select situations, your plan would bog down in minutiae if you created a detailed response for all variations of what might happen. This is particularly true of a complex company like DuPont. When designing our plan, we boiled the scenarios down to just three, based on parameters particular to each of the three groupings.

Key Points for Focusing Your Planning:

☑ Conduct a Vulnerability Assessment (see Chapter 7) to guide your planning.

☑ Do not allow the wide range of vulnerabilities to overwhelm your planning.

☑ Find a few useful groupings of potential crises, using the response parameters as criteria.

On-site Crises—If a crisis were to develop at a DuPont-owned site, some important elements would help define the response. Regardless of the type of crisis at one of the company's manufacturing plants—an industrial accident, a natural disaster, an active shooter, a terrorist attack, or a worker strike—all would have some aspects in common.

Common elements to be counted on at company-owned sites:

   ❋ A fence around the property and other security measures.

   ❋ DuPont employees at the site trained to deal with emergencies.

   ❋ Company-conducted training given to local emergency responders.

   ❋ Site leaders who have relationships with people in the community and who know local government authorities and the local news media.

All of this matters in crisis management.

Off-site Crises— A problem centered at an offsite location alters all of the above. For example, management of a situation in which a DuPont chemical is leaking from a truck on a highway far from one of the company's facilities varies dramatically from the management of the same leak from the same truck at a company site. To deal with a leak at a remote site, hazmat experts and their equipment must travel to the scene. It takes time for them to get to a remote location.

To add to the complications if the company doesn't own the site:

   ❋ DuPont would have no direct authority to cordon off an area.

   ❋ DuPont experts would have no knowledge of the training and skills of the local emergency responders for dealing with a spill.

   ❋ Leaders at DuPont would not know the local government officials or news media, and those people would not know DuPont.

Business/Corporate Crises— Not all crises have a geographic focal point. A product-quality issue, for example, can be spread over a large area. A financial crisis may not have any geographic limitations at all. In many instances, a cyber attack is a virtual crisis. Also, as opposed to the on-site and off-site crises mentioned above, business and corporate crises tend to last much longer and have a wider reach. Again, the different parameters define the response needs.

Depending on the type of business you are in, you may find other groupings more useful. An airline, a hospital, or a bank each will have special vulnerabilities that merit special planning.

5.4 Persistent Crises

I have worked on crises that had tails more than ten years long. While we were not in active crisis management every day during that extended period, people always were working to address aspects that lingered. Often, lingering pieces relate to litigation, but they can include other commitments or dimensions as well. Think of the famous cases of the Exxon Valdez oil spill in Alaska, the Deepwater Horizon oil spill in the Gulf of Mexico, or the Fukushima nuclear disaster in Japan that resulted from the 2011 earthquake and tsunami. While crises may fade from the front pages of the newspapers, they are not gone or forgotten by the people who labor in the aftermath.

Persistent crises tend to fade from public view for periods of time only to rise again. The reemergence can be linked to events such as court trials or anniversaries of the initial event. One common reason for reemergence is that each time a government agency issues a report or performs a regulatory review of the crisis cause and response, the whole saga is revisited. The crisis remains a resource drain on the company throughout the lifetime of the aftermath.

5.5 Letting Go When It's Over

When a crisis has become something of a way of life for an extended period, certain members of the team may find it hard to let go, strange as that may sound. They may have come to enjoy the attention given them by senior management and do not want to go back to their anonymous existences. They also may have become addicted to the periodic adrenaline rush when the persistent crisis spikes anew.

It is not always easy to know when and how to let go. Symptoms to watch for that indicate it may be time to phase down the response effort include over-management of lesser problems and people searching for problems to manage in relation to the former crisis.

If a particular crisis became so problematic at its zenith that a separate team was needed to deal with it, action by senior management may be required to close down the operation when the team members resist moving on after the crisis has been resolved.

Concluding the crisis response may not be as easy or effective as you might imagine. Believe it or not, the team may not want to disband. One option is to replace leaders of the team with people not already associated with the team or the crisis. Another useful technique can be to clearly mark the end with ceremonial recognition of those who contributed. Chapter 16, Section 3 provides details on what to do and what not to do in relation to recognition.

CHAPTER

6

Context of the Crisis

What's In This Chapter:

6.1   Core Values
6.2   Principles
6.3   Public Expectations for Transparency
6.4   Public Expectations for Instant Access

6.1 Core Values

Throughout the years I worked at DuPont, the company's Core Values were very much alive every day. Each meeting started with a "Core Values Contact." Even when the CEO was having a quarterly earnings call with company leaders, the session began with a discussion of how the company was doing on one or more of its Core Values.

A 2013 study by Hill+Knowlton Strategies found that almost half of the American public believes the actions of companies are not aligned with the values they publicly espouse.

DuPont Core Values:

☑ Safety and Health

☑ Environmental Stewardship

☑ Highest Ethics

☑ Respect for People

Because DuPont's Core Values were woven into the day-to-day operations of the company, they formed a solid foundation from which to manage the company's response to any situation. The company's Core Values never shone brighter than during the dark days of a crisis.

When Hurricane Katrina hit the Gulf Coast of the U.S. in late August 2005, DuPont was one of the companies severely impacted by the deadly storm. A number of DuPont manufacturing facilities were damaged, and many employees lost their homes. Because of the lack of communications available throughout the region, we were having great difficulty locating our people to see whether they were all right or in need of help. As we headed into the Labor Day weekend, we still had not located many. During one of our crisis meetings with senior leaders, the CEO leaned forward at the table and said, "I want every possible effort expended to find our people and help them. I do not want to find out next Tuesday that there was something we could have done, but now it's too late. This is dragging on too long. Do everything possible to find and help our people."

Many of us spent that weekend trying every phone number we could while others in the area drove the neighborhoods searching for clues to where our people were. As it turned out, we located every employee, and while all were safe, many were in desperate need of water, food, gasoline, cash, and other basics. DuPont hastened to establish a tent city at one of our facilities in Mississippi to provide shelter, security, food, sanitary facilities, medical care, and other necessities for our people and their families. The company also extended support to others in the community.

While Katrina was an extreme circumstance, the DuPont Core Values were cornerstones in all responses as will be shown in later discussions of the tools for decision making. The Core Values were the basis of all we did in crisis management. When a team was stuck on how to move forward, it was not unusual for someone in the room to ask, "What is the right thing to do?"– meaning let's step back and get our moral bearings.

A company's commitment to its Core Values must be genuine, whether in times of crisis or not. How the company behaves and does business day in and day out creates the foundation for how it will respond during a crisis.

 War Story | **Doing Right Serves a Company Well**

The Tennessee Chamber of Commerce was on record against a piece of legislation for reasons unrelated to gay rights; however, members of the gay community in the state had concerns that one effect of the proposed law would be to allow discrimination. To create pressure, gay activists drew connections to companies— DuPont included—that had managers on the Chamber's board of directors. That approach worked, and DuPont soon found itself drawn into the controversy, replete with allegations that the company was acting to limit gay rights. The story was getting traction in the traditional news media as well as through social media.

DuPont, however, had a Core Value expressing Respect for People, with a performance record to back it up. Because of its history of consistent behavior to support this Core Value, the company had a firm foundation for refuting what was being said. The DuPont Public Affairs and Government Affairs people who were charged with correcting the allegations in Tennessee consulted with the company's BGLAD network (Bisexuals, Gays, Lesbians, Transgenders, and Allies at DuPont) and then quickly took a strong stand in favor of gay rights. The gay activists realized that DuPont was on their side, and they dropped the allegations against the company.

Many companies have Core Values of one sort or another. But two elements must be true for them to add value to a crisis response. First, as noted previously they must be real, not just framed platitudes hanging on a wall for years but never really noticed or consciously followed. At DuPont they were taken seriously, frequently cited, and often put into practice. Violating any of the Core Values was the easiest way to lose a job at DuPont.

The second element is that the Core Values must be bold. While discussing the importance of Core Values with a leader of a prominent retail firm, I was stunned by what he said. He boasted that they too had Core Values. First and foremost, he said, is to obey the law. We were eating lunch together during a crisis management workshop I was giving, and I almost choked on my salad. "Obey the law? Well, there's a stretch goal! Isn't that a given?" I didn't say it, but I sure thought it.

6.2 Principles

Even before the years during which I led global crisis management, DuPont had established a formal set of Crisis Management Principles to guide the company's efforts. The principles were based on the company's Core Values.

Crisis Management Principles

✻ We will act with caring, compassion, and concern.

✻ We will act morally and ethically; laws and regulations will be minimum standards.

✻ We will place the highest priority on human health and safety.

✻ We will ensure our actions are guided by respect for the environment.

✻ We will be open, straightforward, and accessible.

✻ We will consider all stakeholders in our actions— communicating to them fully in a timely way and using normal business channels to the extent possible.

✻ We will acknowledge appropriate responsibility immediately and determine liability after the facts are known.

✻ We will make crisis response a priority over other needs, specifically in regard to the deployment of resources, and ensure employees are trained in crisis response.

These principles from DuPont are bold statements. They served as valuable guideposts through the fog of many a crisis.

Much has been written about the shortcomings of the response to the Deepwater Horizon oil spill in the Gulf of Mexico. I, too, conducted an analysis of the response—not to point a finger, but rather to hold a mirror up to our own crisis management program and ask whether we would have done any better. One thing I can say is that employing our Crisis Management Principles would have yielded a better outcome.

The next to last statement in the list of principles says that DuPont "will acknowledge appropriate responsibility first..." Certainly that statement can make attorneys squirm because in the litigation that follows most crises, that sort of an acknowledgement may make their jobs much harder. But from a holistic crisis management perspective, case studies show it usually is the best approach.

Think of the Ford/Firestone tire controversy that first came to light in 2000. Allegations indicated that certain Ford models, most particularly Ford Explorers, were subject to excessive roll-over risks and further that the risks were related to tire tread separation on particular Firestone tires. Neither company took responsibility for the problems. Instead, each company used its lawyers to assign blame to the other, thus extending the crisis and doing serious damage to their reputations.

When the public and other stakeholders see a company trying to dodge accountability, they receive a significant signal from that. Consider the negative results when Exxon stated that the massive oil spill from the Exxon Valdez tanker in Prince William Sound, Alaska, was really the fault of Exxon Shipping, not the larger corporation. Although technically the blame should have been attributed to Exxon Shipping, to many outsiders, the finger pointing seemed like an attempt to shift accountability.

6.3 Public Expectations for Transparency

The public—especially those people who perceive that they have been directly impacted by your crisis—will watch your behavior closely. They will take signals not only from what you say, but also from what they believe you may be hiding.

Today there are rising expectations that the public has a right to all information regarding your crisis. The paradox here is that often the wider you open the doors, the less people want to come in. They get a signal either way. If you resist providing access to information, people imagine it is because you have something to hide. The reverse is true as well. If the company shows a willingness to openly share information, the public may lose interest.

Unfortunately, it is not as simple as that. There will be adversaries also waiting to gain access to your information. Activists may use your information to spotlight shortcomings. Competitors will comb through your disclosures looking for material that will aid their approach to customers. Plaintiffs' attorneys will see your openness as an easier route than the "discovery" process of the legal system. Moreover, if you have new or different information in your possession later, the plaintiffs' lawyers may argue that any differences are due to intentional deception or other clandestine motives.

 WAR STORY | **Can't be Important if You Called to Tell Us**

While dealing with a difficult product-quality issue, the team assigned to manage the crisis became aware of a previously unknown report showing that somewhere in the company there had been early knowledge of the potential problem. The team debated at some length whether to give the information to key reporters who had been writing about the overall matter. Finally, the decision was made to do so. As it turned out, they weren't interested. Presumably, since we had called to tell them about it, they figured it couldn't be of much importance.

CASE STUDY | **Your Silence is Deafening**

Communications at Penn State University during the child abuse scandal that erupted in November 2011 were universally assessed to range from poor to nonexistent. When the university president was replaced and his successor tried to connect with alumni via town meetings in January 2012, he ran into angry audiences. The New York Times reported on a remark at a meeting in Philadelphia:

"We want to hear from the trustees. We want them to explain why they made the decisions they did. Their silence is just incredible. It just keeps getting worse."

Clearly, the usually loyal alums were getting major signals from the deafening silence.

6.4 Public Expectations for Instant Access

Related to the expectations for transparency are expectations for instant access. People do not expect to wait days or weeks for you to decide whether to share information and then take more time to prepare it for distribution. They do not understand the inner complexities of such tasks and often do not care. When a mother says she wants to see your safety data related to a product-quality issue, she means she wants it now. Her trust in you hangs in the balance. Delays tip the scales toward distrust.

Digital media amplify these expectations. Everything else is available through social media or the Internet, so why, they wonder, can't you just put your information there?

If you cannot share everything requested, indicate why. If you can share it but not yet, tell them that, and tell them why. Simply clamming up sends a bad message. People have a remarkable ability to understand if you take time to give them the reasons you cannot provide all of the information they request. Your reason may be that you are still working to gather the facts and to fully comprehend the situation. If that is all you have to say, then say it, and tell them when you expect to be able to provide the information. If they hear nothing, it is human nature to fill the void with negatives.

....

Statement made during Johnson & Johnson's Extra Strength Tylenol® cyanide poisoning crisis:

"This is the principle we're going to follow. We're going to tell them what we know, and we're not going to tell them what we don't know. We'll tell them we don't know, and we'll get back to them when we do know."

—*Lawrence G. Foster, Public Relations leader*

....

CHAPTER

7

Crisis Planning

What's In This Chapter:

7.1 Crisis Plan
7.2 Vulnerability Assessment
7.3 Response Guides
7.4 Crisis Team
7.5 Annual Planning

7.1 Crisis Plan

Highly efficient and effective, the DuPont Corporate Crisis Plan was referred to as a concept of operations plan. It outlined how all the pieces fit together including who was to perform what role, and it described the structure and function of the various moving parts.

Despite the complexity of the DuPont Company noted in the Preface, the company's crisis plan was barely 40 pages. From that base it was supported by contact lists, checklists, and the like. When a crisis team assembled, team members were reminded to go first to their checklists, which were never more than two pages.

When I gave a talk at a crisis management seminar conducted by the International Association of Business Communicators a few years ago, you can imagine my surprise to hear one crisis "expert" there not only advocate for creating a thick, 3-ring-binder crisis plan, but that he went on to say when a crisis starts, each team member should read the first 50 pages to reacquaint themselves with the plan. I knew immediately that the guy never had managed crises in the real world. In the rapid-fire arena of today's business world, you cannot have the entire team sit down to read 50 pages before beginning a crisis response.

If the person tasked with developing your firm's crisis plan never has created one, you should look for a qualified consultant. Be aware, though, that most PR firms, as well as many law firms, security consultants, and others will tell you they can create such a plan for your company. Be skeptical. Ask for references and contact them. Do not just ask whether the consultant helped them create a plan—ask whether the plan is actually used and how effective it is when a crisis erupts. A 4-inch-thick, 3-ring binder that sits on the shelf during an actual crisis is of little value.

Outline for a Crisis Management Plan

* **Scope–** Description of what is covered by this plan.

* **Crisis Definition–** Our definition of a crisis.

* **Core Values and Principles–** High-level guides for behavior during a crisis.

* **Roles and Responsibilities–** List of key personnel and groups with a brief description of their roles before and during a crisis.

* **Groupings of Crises–** Categories of crises based on the parameters common to certain types of situations.

* **Activation Levels–** Process for response through a defined number of activation levels along with criteria that move the response to the next level.

* **Systems–** Brief descriptions of the basic systems that support crisis planning and response.

* **Facilities and Equipment–** Descriptions and basic guides for the infrastructure that supports crisis response.

* **Training and Plan Maintenance–** Approach to regular training, plan upgrades and testing.

* Appendices

  * **Response Guides–** One-page guides that list the key

elements of response to high probability crises.

- **Checklists–** Simple guides for use during an activation.

- **Contact lists–** Names of team members and alternates with their contact information.

7.2 Vulnerability Assessment

Conducting a formal Vulnerability Assessment is a good initial step in creating a well-crafted crisis plan. You first want to know: What are we planning for?

A comprehensive vulnerability assessment involves a formal survey to ask selected employees across a diagonal slice of the organization what current or future threats concern them. At the same time, you can ask how well prepared they believe the organization is.

The type of business you are in helps determine your vulnerabilities to crises. If you are in the trucking business, you should be thinking about accidents, delayed shipments, or labor strikes. If you are in the fresh vegetable business, you should be thinking about product contamination, crop diseases, and, like those in the trucking business, delayed shipments.

Of course, some threats loom commonly over many types of businesses. As has been stated, natural disasters can strike almost any company. A financial crisis, a pandemic, or a cyber attack can threaten essentially any business from the local convenience store to a mega retailer to a diversified multinational corporation.

A vulnerability assessment can be conducted for any or all levels of the organization. It could be done, for example, for just one warehouse facility, or it could be done for the entire corporation. All levels are valid—and needed. The warehouse should focus on the concerns at that level, such as severe weather or labor issues. At the business level, the team should assess potential product or supply-chain issues. At the corporate level, the questions should involve topics such as executive succession, geopolitical turmoil, financial crises, hostile takeovers, and other broad areas.

The vulnerability assessment needs the visible support of the top business leader. This executive should send a communication to those who will be surveyed asking them to be honest and open in their views. To help with the candor, the input should be compiled in a fashion that maintains confidentiality regarding who offered what suggestions.

How you conduct the survey matters a great deal. A vulnerability assessment is best conducted by an outside firm. For one reason, it is hard to carve out the time for internal staff to do the work. Secondly, while it is not overly complicated, experience matters. Because you don't want a novice learning how to do the survey on your project, hiring a company that has done assessments previously is helpful.

Perhaps most important is that, by using an outside firm you are likely to get a more candid and objective review of the vulnerabilities. Candid, because senior leaders are more likely to air their deepest worries to an independent consultant than to a junior employee. Objective, because a fresh set of eyes can spot potential problems that a longtime employee no longer notices. People become accepting and even blind to risks that have been there for years.

A Vulnerability Assessment questionnaire

A Vulnerability Assessment can be conducted using general or specific questions. Here are some sample general questions:

- ✱ What is your definition of a crisis?
- ✱ Do you have a crisis management plan?
- ✱ Do you have a defined crisis team?
- ✱ Has your unit responded to any crises?
- ✱ How did the team do?
- ✱ What worked well?
- ✱ What did they miss?
- ✱ What did they learn?
- ✱ Do you ever practice response to a crisis?
- ✱ Thinking broadly, what types of issues or crises do you

think might befall your organization?

✱ When you project five or ten years into the future, how does that perspective change?

✱ From the list(s) of potential issues or crises, what are your top concerns?

✱ Plotting potential issues or crises on a graph of probability versus severity of impact, which ones rate a high/high?

While a face-to-face discussion using a third-party is highly preferable, don't give up if you cannot go that route. If budget or other constraints dictate that an outside consultant cannot be used, there are other ways to get the work done. For example, SurveyMonkey or similar electronic tools—most of them readily available online—can be used to conduct a survey that is likely to elicit open and reliable answers when it, too, is constructed so that the input is anonymous except to the person who compiles the data. The compiled information can then be used to guide a discussion among key personnel.

The next step involves narrowing down the list of vulnerabilities. In Chapter 5, Section 3, I describe how, despite the complexity of the DuPont Company, we coalesced the vulnerabilities into three groupings: On-site, Off-site, and Business/Corporate. The categories were based on the parameters common for certain types of crises.

For an on-site crisis, the plan addressed incidents that could happen at one of the company's facilities. It wouldn't matter whether the crisis was a natural disaster, an industrial accident, or a terrorist attack. The important factors would be the same. For an off-site situation, such as a rail or truck accident, the company would need to mobilize resources to that scene. Beyond on-site and off-site crises, everything else fell into the business/corporate bucket. Those crises tend not to be narrowly focused in any specific geography. Product-quality problems, a pandemic, a cyber attack, or a financial crisis are all examples of problems that fall into the latter grouping.

The three groupings were outlined in the plan at the corporate level. For any sub-team of the corporate crisis program, their plan could move to the next level of detail. For example, the Supply

Chain team might think about three other groupings:

1. Direct Impacts

✻ A natural disaster (e.g., a tornado) hits a company manufacturing or distribution center.

✻ An industrial accident (e.g., a fire) occurs at a company manufacturing or distribution center.

✻ A product-quality issue within the company causes a stop-sale and/or a recall.

2. Indirect Impacts

✻ A natural disaster, terrorist attack, or other disruption plays havoc with the distribution infrastructure (e.g., a railroad bridge is out or a port is shut down).

✻ An issue related to critical-material supply results in unreliable or delayed shipments and, in turn, disruption of manufacturing or delivery of products to customers.

3. Combination of Direct and Indirect

✻ A major natural disaster (e.g., a hurricane or an earthquake) causes widespread infrastructure problems as well as damage to company facilities, and possibly also renders a significant percentage of employees unable to work.

✻ A pandemic creates worldwide disruption of systems of all sorts lasting many months with sporadic spikes of intensity in any particular locale.

In the Direct category, the ball is largely in the company's court. That does not necessarily make the matter easier to resolve, but it does provide control over some parameters. In the Indirect category, the outcome may be more in the hands of outside parties. The Combination category is likely the worst scenario.

Key Point:

☑ It is essential to keep your list of vulnerabilities simplified. Find ways to group the risks based on the parameters that will define the response.

7.3 Response Guides

If your vulnerability assessment points to some specific, high probability/high impact threats, you should consider creating Response Guides for them as supplements to your overall crisis plan.

An obvious example is that an airline will want to be prepared for a plane crash. In a response guide you can outline the high priority initial tasks that must be completed and who is going to do them. Who drafts your core communications content? What is the approval process? Who serves as corporate spokesperson? Who posts information on your website and what is the process for engaging on social media? Who monitors traditional media and social media? Who goes to the scene?

All of this can and should be decided well in advance of an actual crisis. Chapter 8, Section 3 addresses crisis exercises. Your Response Guide for a given scenario should be used in practice sessions to test how well it works and to evaluate whether it is adequate.

7.4 Crisis Team

In an organization that is relatively small, a standing crisis team can be established to address most types of crises. For example, if you operate a community hospital, the number of players usually is limited, so creating a team is rather straightforward.

In a more complicated organization, team creation is not so simple. Structuring for crisis response is covered in greater detail later, but for the moment here are some important considerations.

Your approach to a crisis team must be holistic. That is, every crucial function should be represented. This is not to say that for every crisis a person from each staff department must come sit in the room. "Selective Activation" should be the norm. If a company has a truck leaking a chemical at a truck stop, there probably is no need for the IT leader to be in the room. Conversely, if there is a hacker attack on the company's financial systems, there probably is no need to mobilize the hazmat team.

Every person on the crisis team must have at least one designated alternate. For DuPont, in most cases there were two alternates. It is a fairly easy task to designate the two alternates on a calm day before there is a crisis. That is when it should be done. It is far more difficult and distracting during a crisis to find that the first two designees for one role are out of pocket and cannot respond to deal with the crisis. It is then up for grabs as to who should jump in. Moreover, that new person will not have been trained and is likely to function like the proverbial deer in the headlights.

7.5 Annual Planning

Creating a strategic program at the beginning of each year, along with a rolling five-year outlook, allows you to ensure that you are moving your overall program forward. This practice also creates an opportunity for you to review the program with your senior leaders and discuss any gaps or needs.

Across the top of a large chart, list the months for the coming year, the quarters for the next year, followed by a yearly view for the remaining three years. Down the left column, list major work areas such as training, crisis team exercises, planning, systems and facilities upgrades, and meetings. Inside the boxes in your grid, place brief notations about what each item entails.

If you have project management software to help with your planning, that is an enhancement. Lacking that, though, the more important point is that you take the time to do the planning. In some ways, having the strategic program as a visual on a paper chart in your crisis room, if you have a designated facility, is actually an asset because it keeps the year's plans in front of everyone.

....

"Plans are nothing; planning is everything."
—Dwight D. Eisenhower

....

CHAPTER

8

Crisis Preparedness

What's In This Chapter:

8.1 Resources
8.2 Training
8.3 Exercises

8.1 Resources

Just as smokejumpers plan their resource needs before heading out to fight a fire, you must consider the resources you will need for responding to a crisis. If you operate in an area of heavy winter storms, what resources will you need to prevent disruption of your operations? If you are in the food business and have a concern about contamination and foodborne illness, do you have the diagnostic equipment needed to quickly trace a potential problem?

The starting point for such considerations is your vulnerability assessment. Your resources begin at the basic level. Where will your team assemble? You likely do not need a war room that looks like it belongs at the Pentagon. Simply designating a specific conference room as your crisis room often will suffice. While it will remain in service most days as a regular meeting room, you want to make sure it also has the supplies and equipment needed for responding to a crisis. Chapter 9, Section 3 provides a checklist of items to consider.

The cost of needed resources can mount quickly. But do not

assume that you need to buy everything. You just need access to the equipment and services. Get creative.

* How else might you obtain resources you need without spending lots of money?

* Do you have to own them?

* If you don't have the resources you will need in-house, where can you get them quickly?

* Who else will be scrambling for those same resources when disaster strikes, and how can you assure access to them?

8.2 Training

Training takes various forms depending on the crises you are preparing for. The most basic form of training is teaching people about your plan and how the crisis program works. Giving preparedness training should be a regular endeavor. People will move off or onto the crisis team, and all team members—new as well as experienced personnel—need regular reminders and reinforcement to remain up-to-speed. Basic training can be offered via a webinar to conserve travel costs. For a large organization, classes can be set up at regular times each year. Remember to accommodate for time zones if you have team members in different parts of the world.

You also may need to arrange specialized types of training for response to particular types of crises. Your crisis response may demand use of equipment to diagnose the problem or to mitigate the impacts. You will want to make sure that qualified individuals are available to maintain and use the equipment anytime the need arises.

Another type of training involves learning from the real-world experiences of your own organization or others. Chapter 17 describes the importance of conducting debriefs after crises. These efforts provide great training opportunities for the team.

After the 2009 H1N1 pandemic, we implemented a worldwide debrief process at DuPont and then provided the results to senior leadership as well as to the other crisis teams. We highlighted effective elements of the response to the crisis and also cited areas for improvement.

To capture some key lessons, learn from your own experiences, but also take time to analyze crises that do not involve your company. After the tragic shootings at Virginia Tech in 2007, we looked at how their communications system worked, and we found areas where we could accelerate our own processes. In relation to the handling of the 2010 Deepwater Horizon oil spill, we looked at both the crisis management approach and the process stewardship aspects. In the wake of the Penn State sex abuse scandal that came to light in 2011, we examined problems in their crisis response and crisis communications. Likewise we looked at the General Motors recalls of 2014 and the Sony cyber attacks that happened at the end of that year. We learned something of value from each of those difficult situations, and that is the whole point of analyzing the experiences and outcomes of others in crisis.

The news media report on some crisis every single day. Chipotle, Volkswagen, Wells Fargo, Samsung—the line moves fast. Although in a few years people may barely recall any details of specific crises, those real-time situations are ready-made opportunities to educate your team. It doesn't matter whether a crisis occurs in politics, sports, the entertainment industry, or in an area closely related to your field. The general concepts are the same. Assess the responses to those crises and discuss the analysis with your team. Look at what the organizations did well and what you might have done differently. Challenge your team so they are positioned to do better. Moreover, by spotlighting the most current and prominent crises, you keep your team energized.

8.3 Exercises

They say that practice makes perfect. I am not sure there is such a thing as a perfect crisis response, but I do know that practice certainly improves performance. Although there are a number of ways to practice crisis response, two of the most common are the full-blown crisis drill and the tabletop exercise.

Crisis Drills

In common parlance, a crisis drill is a practice session where the parts are actively moving. If you are testing evacuation of a workplace, you are actually moving employees and visitors out of the facility. If you are testing a shelter-in-place technique at a school, you assemble the children in their safe zones. You won't really know how—or whether—your plans will work until you try them.

 War Story | **Never Underestimate a Parent**

Prior to working for DuPont, I was deputy director of the National Institute for Chemical Studies in Charleston, West Virginia. Because of that role, I served as an officer in the Kanawha Valley Emergency Preparedness Council—now known as the Kanawha Putnam Emergency Planning Committee—a premier organization that has guided preparedness for emergencies for many years. As required by its charter, KPEPC regularly conducts drills to challenge their response capabilities and find any gaps.

While I was part of the organization, we conducted a drill that simulated what would happen during a shelter-in-place at a local elementary school. The hypothetical scenario was a toxic chemical release in the vicinity. Local chemical companies participated in the drill along with all of the emergency responders in the community.

I was an observer inside the school, where everything went according to plan up to a point. What had not been anticipated, though, was how parents would react when they saw fire trucks arrive at the school. Because the team had failed to tell parents about the drill, mothers and fathers came in droves to "rescue" their kids.

We learned two important lessons at the school that day. First, you must let those in the broader circle who are closely connected to the "victims" know what you are doing. That lapse was obvious and easily fixed. The second lesson was that in a real emergency, people are going to do whatever they can to assure the safety of their loved ones and friends. How to manage that dynamic is more complex, and it is exactly the sort of problem you want to highlight before a real crisis occurs.

A crisis drill requires months of planning and preparation. Usually the timing is announced in advance so that it is on the calendars of key people and so that you can warn others that a practice session will be happening. Of course conducting an unannounced drill creates a more realistic situation, but participation of key players may be limited due to prior commitments.

 WAR STORY | **A Real-World Crisis During a Drill**

A good crisis drill scenario injects all kinds of surprise developments, so it could be difficult to know whether a new piece of information was part of the drill or was a real crisis unfolding during the exercise. When I participated in a DuPont training drill before I became the crisis leader, the outside firm hired to design and conduct the scenario wisely had factored in what we would do in the event a real crisis occurred while we were in practice mode.

We had been working through the drill for a number of hours when a call came in that some of the senior leaders would have to leave because a real-world event in the Middle East demanded immediate attention. The man leading the drill used a previously arranged code to signal all participants that the practice exercise was being interrupted in order to address a real crisis.

 WAR STORY | **Oops, They Didn't Really Die**

During a drill there are lots of moving parts, with people doing some of the things they actually would do during a real-life crisis. Phone calls are placed and answered; emails are sent; requests for information may go to people not directly working on the drill.

Because the circle expands to a broader group, it is crucial that all communications, verbal and written, begin and end with a statement indicating, "This is a drill." When the adrenaline is flowing and the scenario feels real, it is easy to forget to add those words.

During one crisis drill at DuPont, the scenario involved a hypothetical industrial accident. In order to practice upward communication, one task was to update senior leaders who were not part of the exercise. One of the crisis team members sent an email to some top brass indicating that 44 people were dead as a result of an accident at a company plant in Tennessee. Unfortunately, he forgot to include the "This is a drill" notice on the email.

Luckily, the person on the receiving end of the transmission thought to confirm the facts before acting on them. No harm done, but it was an important reminder that drills are not without their own risks.

If designed and executed well, a drill can do a remarkable job of simulating the feel of a real crisis, clear down to getting your adrenaline flowing. A good drill is intended not only to be realistic but also to push the limits of the team. The purpose is to find gaps in your plan and to highlight areas for improvement.

For realism, you need a knowledgeable person who will not be participating in the drill to help write the scenario. Attention to the details of the scenario, which should be kept secret from the team being tested, is important. Unless you get the details right, some of the participants will struggle. Having elements that don't fit together well or that never could happen make it hard for the participants to believe in the scenario.

Tabletop Exercises

A tabletop exercise is a simpler and less time-consuming way to test the crisis management program. A tabletop exercise is a scenario-based discussion among the members of one or more crisis teams. It provides an opportunity to explore how teams would function when dealing with a real-world situation, but without actually implementing the actions.

Like any other crisis drill, a high-quality tabletop exercise typically requires at least two months of preparation as well as early notification of all team members. The point at which you announce the exercise is a good time to enlist management's visible support. If the boss sends out the announcement, it carries extra clout and sets the expectation that everyone will be there.

When put into motion, a tabletop exercise normally takes two to four hours. Ideally, when the "crisis" begins, team members assemble in their crisis rooms, although people can participate by phone or video conference.

The primary goal of a tabletop exercise is to allow open discussion of the workings of the crisis team or teams. By talking through a scenario, team members assess how they would respond in that specific situation. They also discuss how they would interact with other parts of the organization. The result is that they discover elements that would work well and also define ways to upgrade the crisis response.

A second goal of a tabletop exercise is to energize the team and build support for crisis preparedness. To ensure the practice session is taken seriously and will yield measurable results, nothing sets the tone like the big boss showing up and being clearly focused on the crisis scenario. The rest of the team immediately realizes that they, too, must give the exercise their full attention.

Try to add something in the scenario for each participant. For example, if the finance manager is participating, add some details specific to that manager's function.

Check and double check the details and the timing. Scenarios can have overlapping plot lines, but you need to make sure they all hold together. Finally, adding photos, videos, or fact sheets contributes to the "reality" of the experience.

An ancillary benefit of conducting a tabletop exercise—or any kind of scheduled crisis exercise—is that the deadline alone provides the impetus to review and update the crisis plan, checklists, contact lists, and other resources. The DuPont Corporate Crisis Management Plan required each team to conduct at least one exercise each year, thus also fulfilling the company requirement to update all plans annually. Team leaders were pleased that they were able to address two requirements at one time.

CHAPTER

9

Facilities and Systems

What's In This Chapter:

9.1 Alert System
9.2 Redundancies
9.3 War Room
9.4 Computer Systems

9.1 Alert System

How quickly you can mobilize your crisis team will determine how quickly you can get into action. Any time wasted in mobilizing cuts into the speed with which you can determine the facts, assess your resource needs, and evaluate options for responding to a crisis. In a small organization, a traditional phone-tree approach may work. It needs to be practiced and must be kept up to date. Be aware, though, that you may not have the luxury of the time it takes a couple people to dial the numbers to reach your team members and then have a brief conversation with each of them.

For larger or more complex organizations an automatic notification system is a smart investment. An automatic system allows you to contact your team members rapidly. The system dials all numbers listed for each individual and also will send them text and email messages. Additionally, there are lots of bells and whistles offered in conjunction with an automated alert process. Many systems can keep track of your checklists and log your team's actions during a response. Some systems also can handle external notifications during an incident.

Dozens of companies offer crisis notification services with a range of services and prices. It is wise to do a good assessment up front before signing on with a service firm, because once you start with a company, it is not easy to switch. For example, familiarizing everyone on your teams with the new notification processes requires an investment of their time and attention. In addition, loading contact information into the system can take considerable work. Spend the time to pick a good system at the outset. Be aware, though, that it can be overwhelming to try to evaluate all of the service companies. Because the technologies and companies are changing constantly, it is not possible to provide a review here, but you can get a jump on the process by finding current reviews online.

 WAR STORY | **Rapid Activation During the Pandemic**

DuPont used an automatic notification system that was administered by an outside vendor. We routinely practiced alerting the crisis management teams to ensure they knew what to do if they got an emergency call. That training proved vital when the H1N1 flu pandemic began in 2009.

We had been closely tracking H1N1 developments in Mexico for a few days, but they had not yet reached the level at which we wanted to activate our teams. That point came on the following Saturday. I happened to be in a cabin on a mountain in West Virginia when we became convinced that H1N1 was the real thing, and we needed to activate. I was able to launch our entire program using my smart phone to trigger the notification system. With a custom voice message sent to all team leaders, I announced that we would be holding a conference call the next day.

During the global call on Sunday, we advised all teams that the plans we had developed were to be implemented. One element involved communication with employees. We wanted them to view the company as a reliable source of information and support, and we had prepared to move swiftly in that direction. On Monday, when DuPont employees arrived at work, they immediately saw communications from the company regarding the threat. We effectively implemented a rapid launch of our response program worldwide despite the intervening weekend because of our ability to reach all crisis teams simultaneously.

9.2 Redundancies

If Murphy's Law is ever in play, it is during a crisis. Something will go wrong, and you must be prepared to address the added challenge. For all crucial parts of your system, you need to have alternative means to accomplish every task.

The alert system you select should have backup processes built in. But what if they all fail? You must be ready to contact your team by some other means, which might involve a phone tree, a public address system, radio transmitters, or some other technique.

 War Story | **Crisis on Top of Crisis**

One episode in our response to the double whammy of hurricanes Katrina and Rita in late summer 2005 shows how much can go wrong all at one time. We were dealing with fourteen company facilities along the Gulf Coast that either were damaged or were down because of the successive storms, and numerous employees had suffered severe damage to or total loss of their homes. Just when I thought things couldn't get worse, I got the call from hell: our primary Data Center had gone down. It is important to note that the Data Center is not located anywhere near the Gulf Coast. Even with triple redundancy of electrical power, all systems had crashed hard. We were without our databases and even without the ability to send email.

If the power goes out, what are your alternatives? If the digital phones fail, do you have analog lines? If the cell towers are overloaded—a common problem during a geographically focused crisis—what will you do?

What if you cannot get to your crisis room, for example, during a natural disaster? How can you work with your team? Is virtual assembly possible? If so, is it sufficient? Do you have conference-calling, web-meeting, or video-hookup capabilities?

DuPont's primary crisis management rooms were located at corporate headquarters. If we could not assemble there, alternate facilities were nearby. In the event that the whole area was to be evacuated, a ninety-minute drive would get us to a company facility where senior leaders could eat, sleep, and stay for an extended period. The alternate crisis management center was outfitted with backup power and other capabilities so that we could function in almost any situation.

 War Story | **Planning Based on a Faulty Assumption**

If an evacuation of northern Delaware meant that our senior leaders had to set up shop elsewhere, they would make the ninety-minute drive from headquarters in Wilmington to a conference center on Maryland's Eastern Shore of the Chesapeake Bay. We had been assured that no storm would hit northern Delaware and also strike that part of the Eastern Shore. Hurricane Irene, in 2011, proved that planning assumption to be wrong. The massive storm knocked out power in major parts of the Mid-Atlantic area, including northern Delaware and along the Eastern Shore. Fortunately, we did not have to evacuate, and DuPont was spared major impacts. Nonetheless, we had been alerted to a gap in our redundancy planning. Emergency power generation was installed at our alternative location in Maryland.

Key Point:

....

 All Critical Resources must have a backup arrangement. Creative approaches can be cost effective.

....

CASE STUDY | Small Company, Big Payoff

I once stopped at a local electrical-supply company to pick up some materials for a project I was doing at home. I recall thinking at the time that there was something special about the place. From the moment I walked in, I recognized that it was well designed and customer friendly. It was a pleasant shopping experience, but I did not think much more about it until a few months later when a tornado struck the area and that company's facility was badly damaged.

As it turned out, the electrical-supply company had a crisis management plan in place. Tornadoes are rare in our area, but that company had a plan for what they would do if for any reason their facility sustained serious damage, rendering them unable to operate normally for a period of time. They knew where and how they were going to establish temporary operations and what it would take to get back up and running in the new location.

Because they had a crisis plan, they were back in business quickly, serving their customers even during difficult times.

Some basic planning, which does not need to cost a great deal of money, can serve you well when a disaster happens. Planning for your redundancies is an opportunity for creativity.

9.3 War Room

Each crisis team needs to have its own room in which to assemble and work. Again, it does not have to be an elaborate set-up. It can be a conference room or even a lunch room that has some basic resources.

When you conduct your crisis exercises, make sure you do them in the room where you intend to meet during an actual crisis. You may find shortcomings that can be fixed easily in the calm before the real storm. Here's a checklist of some considerations and resources you might want for your room.

> ✱ **Access control–** During a crisis, it is best to have a room that can be secured so that only team members have access. That way you can keep sensitive notes on the boards and not worry about others seeing them.

> ✱ **Power–** Make sure you have backup power in the event of an outage. Also, make sure you have sufficient outlets for the people who will bring equipment that either needs to be plugged in or must be recharged periodically.

> ✱ **Connectivity–** Consider what landlines or wireless capabilities you will need. Test them regularly to make sure they are still active and that they are compatible with the equipment of the team members.

> ✱ **Printers, copiers, and related equipment–** Make sure you have ready access to printers, copiers, and scanners and that your computers are updated with the latest drivers.

> ✱ **Technical Support–** Know who you will call in the event of system problems. Know who is available 24/7/365.

✱ **Telephones–** Do not rely only on cell phones as your means of voice communications. In the event of a local disaster, some or all of those lines likely will be overloaded or even knocked out of service. You need at least one other mode for voice communication. Talk to your service provider about various scenarios that could interrupt service and plan for your needs.

✱ **Conference call capability–** For conference calls, you will need at least a basic system for speaker-phone capability. Arrange in advance for dial-in numbers that will work for people in whatever parts of the world you operate.

✱ **Video conference capability–** Video conferencing can be useful, especially for certain types of situations, such as when multiple teams in multiple locations are working on the same problem. Assess your needs and match them to your available budget. Capabilities can range from a simple webcam on a laptop to a full-blown multifunctional system.

✱ **Projector and Screen–** An electronic projector, a screen, and a sound system often are needed for sharing and working on documents in the crisis room. Because time is of the essence when dealing with a crisis there is no excuse for not being prepared. I have seen a great deal of time lost simply trying to get an image on the screen. Someone on the team should be trained in connecting the projector display. If you will need to connect laptops to the projector, be sure you have the cables you will need. Keep spare batteries for the remote control in your supplies cabinet.

✱ **Whiteboards and Chart Pads–** Keeping track of action lists and other work of the team is crucial. You should have at least two whiteboards or chart pads in your crisis room.

✱ **Television–** How will you monitor and record television coverage? While a television screen does not necessarily need to be in your crisis room, you may want to have the capability. You will need a transmission connection of some sort to get the signals.

✱ **Clock and calendar–** A clock and a calendar are basic needs that are not always present but should be. Having an extra clock that can be reset easily to a different time zone is also helpful when working on an incident in another region or another country.

❊ Supplies– You should have a locked cabinet of supplies in your room. Things you want to have available during a crisis have a tendency to disappear between events. Keep a stash of pens, markers, tape, scissors, tablets, push pins, chart pad paper, staplers, paper clips, sticky notes, batteries, electrical extensions, and other items you may need.

❊ Reference materials–If your computer systems go down, how will you access your plans, checklists, and contact lists? Paper is not an outdated technology when it comes to crisis management. Keeping a paper copy of your current plan in your locked cabinet can be an excellent backup system. In addition, if there are crucial technical materials that must be accessed, you should store a copy. You should also consider atlases of the areas where you operate.

❊ The walls– In addition to your whiteboards and flipcharts, your walls can be used to display maps, your crisis management principles, and other relevant–but not confidential–materials. Be sure to have evacuation procedures posted since there may be visitors who are not familiar with the building.

❊ Food and refreshments– A crisis sometimes can run into long and odd hours. Keep a file of vendor information so that you can order coffee, soft drinks and food to sustain your team during a crisis or drill. If possible, find some vendors who operate 24/7/365. Vending machines can also be a backup option.

❊ Waste management and cleaning– If your room has controlled access, that probably means the cleaning staff cannot get in. You will need to make other arrangements. For sensitive documents that you do not need to keep, consider having a good shredder available.

As stated previously, if you are on a limited budget, be creative in how you fulfill your basic needs. You also should prioritize those needs and address the most pressing items first.

9.4 Computer Systems

Highly sophisticated and complicated systems are available for crisis planning and management. Perhaps they are helpful for some organizations, but I never found much need or use for them. Often the biggest drawback is that complicated systems can be a barrier for the average team members who do not use them on a regular basis.

This is not to say computer systems that track the functionality of an organization are not crucial. For example, an electric power company necessarily relies heavily on its computers during a crisis to track its progress in restoring electric power and to communicate with customers.

The comments in the first paragraph are directed at the crisis management systems some vendors offer. A useful alternative to convoluted systems is a simple electronic team room where you can store all critical information: plans, contact lists, checklists, and any basic materials. A good approach is to establish a new, situation-specific team room for each significant crisis. This is in addition to the electronic team room where you store all basic materials on an ongoing basis. In each of the situation-specific team rooms, you can house your most current press statements, Q&A lists, and situation updates, but restrict access to only those who need to go there.

CHAPTER

10

When a Crisis Strikes

What's In This Chapter:

10.1 The "Oh #%&*!" Meeting

Despite your best efforts at crisis prevention, your worst fears can become reality. A crisis occurs, and it's time for action. You must lead the team that is about to parachute into the smoke of an unfolding crisis. Your overarching function as the crisis team leader is to harness the energy of the team, gather the critical information, get the team lined up to act on the highest priorities, and monitor the progress of the crisis response to determine whether it is proving to be effective or whether other strategies need to be employed. The clock is ticking.

Your first step as the crisis team leader is to use the alert system to contact the team members and tell them to assemble in the crisis room. Perhaps you have to boot the folks who thought they had the room reserved for a regular meeting. You unlock the supplies cabinet and bring out the materials you had stored there for just this moment: checklists, contact lists, whiteboard markers, and more.

It is important to be braced for the dynamics of this first meeting. As you dial up the conference-call number to accommodate those who could not be there in person and you watch others file into the room, consider all of the emotions that are beginning to swirl. Some folks are anxious to understand what is happening, but a few are aggravated that you interrupted their day. Others probably believe you are overreacting. Someone may be arriving with an even greater burden—perhaps knowledge that in some fashion he or she had a hand in triggering the problem.

 War Story | **Nobody is Going to Jail**

During one product crisis, we had to deal with a critical regulatory compliance situation because the company missed the deadline for providing a required report to the government. It was an honest error, but it was an error nonetheless, and a penalty would be paid.

We were agonizing over some of the details in the midst of our fourth meeting about this problem when the attorney on the team made a passing remark about the size of the fine we would have to pay. Suddenly, the product manager held up her hand and said, "Stop! Repeat what you just said."

The attorney repeated that we likely would be facing a fine in the hundreds of thousands of dollars. "What about jail?" the product manager wanted to know.

"Jail?" the attorney replied. "Nobody is going to jail. This is a civil violation. We will pay a fine, file the report, and make sure it doesn't happen again. End of story. Nobody said anything about jail."

The product manager choked back tears. For several days she had been living in dread of having to go to jail because her business had failed to comply with the law.

The important lessons learned from this situation:

Be clear in all communications about an incident, even within the team. In this instance, the product manager never had been in that type of situation and didn't know that when the attorney referred to the violation as a civil matter, the extent of the penalty would be a fine. This violation was not a criminal matter that might involve incarceration.

Be attuned to the feelings and needs of each individual on the team. People may be carrying burdens you are unaware of. I can only imagine the anguish of that manager as she worried for days about something that was not even a possibility.

The first meeting of the group can be tumultuous. The meeting might include a torrent of emotions from a boss who is in denial or the meltdown of a panic-stricken underling who perhaps should not have been included on the crisis team in the first place.

Key Points: Get Started on the Right Foot

☑ Ready.....Go!
  - Write an agenda on the board (Chapter 12, Section 3)
  - Address good records management
  - Analyze the situation using the Box your Thoughts tool
  - Begin designating team members
  - Agree on a spokesperson
  - Assign a person to develop a standby statement
  - Create a list of Action Items
  - Schedule next meetings

10.2 Your First Audience – Consider the Needs of Those in the Room

The first concern of a crisis team leader relates to the needs of the people in the crisis room. Some of the details are basic. If it's around lunch time, make plans to feed the troops lest they become even more agitated and cranky than they already are. If it's late in the day, check to see whether there are people who need to pick up their kids from daycare by 6 p.m.

 War Story | **Skipping Meals—Not a Sweet Idea**

During one crisis, I learned a tough lesson about making sure the basic needs of the team are addressed. We had spent the morning wrestling with some difficult aspects of a situation, and the time slipped past the lunch hour.

Although I had worked with one particular man for years, I had no idea that he was diabetic. Suddenly, Mike stood up and rushed from the room. I didn't know why he bolted and thought little of it until I heard commotion out in the hallway. Mike had hung on as long as he could but finally knew he had to get to the vending machine to immediately consume something that contained sugar. Unfortunately, he did not get there in time; instead, he collapsed outside the door. Workers who saw him fall had no idea what was going on and summoned medical help.

Mike recovered, but I swore that I would never let that happen again. I became adamant about not letting a team work through mealtime without providing something for people to eat.

The first meeting, when the process for understanding the situation and planning the response begins, can be the most chaotic. Often extra people are present. That's usually all right, unless the situation is so sensitive that only a select few should be privy to the details. Who stays on the team can be addressed later.

10.3 Records Management

The first advice to the assembled team, even before beginning to assess the situation at hand, is about records management. It's helpful to have the attorney deliver this message because sooner or later, especially in the U.S., a crisis usually involves litigation. Any notes people take may need to be preserved. It is a good idea for the attorney to provide guidance at the outset on how information should be recorded and by whom.

10.4 Situation Assessment—Box your Thoughts

Next, adding structure to the first meeting will assist in calming the people and getting an efficient process started. How to provide that structure will be discussed in greater detail in Chapter 12, Section 3, but in brief, one person should be asked to provide the overview of the situation, lest it quickly descend into bedlam. Others likely will want to chime in, but designating one person to give the basics allows the meeting to begin with a rudimentary structure.

Before the start of the overview, draw headers for five columns on the whiteboard: Positive Points, Critical Unknowns, Key Vulnerabilities, Stakeholders, and Time Drivers. Tell the group that while they listen to the situation being described, you want them to consider that all of the important information will fall into one of the five columns and to flag it as they hear it so you can note it on the board. Most of the information easily will fit into one of the columns, but be aware that for some of it, the decision as to which one won't always be clear cut.

Tool: Box Your Thoughts

☑ "Box Your Thoughts" during the Situation Overview
  • Positive Points
  • Critical Unknowns
  • Key Vulnerabilities
  • Stakeholders
  • Time Drivers

Positive Points– These are items the team will highlight in the Core Statement. The core statement will be discussed further in Chapter 13, Section 4, but in brief, it is an overview of the situation, including what happened and what you are going to do about it. The positive points will be central to this statement. In many cases the positive points you cite will be obvious. For example, if you already have a team of trained professionals addressing the incident, that clearly is a positive point.

Another positive point may not necessarily sound very positive at first. For example, someone might angrily say: "I don't know how the hell this could have happened. We're supposed to have a process to prevent this sort of thing."

Okay, we have a process directly related to this occurrence. That means what happened was a deviation from what we had intended. We then can cite the variant circumstance as an outlier.

Let's say a patient in a hospital was given a unit of contaminated blood. In the Core Statement, part of the message might sound like this: "We have a clearly defined process to prevent this type of situation from happening. Obviously, a mistake has been made. We will determine what went wrong and take measures to ensure that it does not happen again."

You will have defined another positive point, calmed an angry team member, and shown how to create a Core Statement that could become the basis for an announcement to keep stakeholders and the press informed early-on when not a lot of facts are known.

Critical Unknowns– Invariably, there are many things that are unknowns at the outset. List them all on the whiteboard as they are brought up, but do not make the mistake of thinking they are all of equal importance or urgency or that they all merit action. Some are more important than others. Each should be assessed carefully before action is taken to obtain the information.

Key Point: Distracted by the Wrong Details

☑ If I am about to be struck by a bus, one unknown may be whether the bus is running on schedule. It is of some interest because, if the bus is not on schedule, I might not be positioned in front of it at this moment. Despite being an unknown of relevance, it is not critical to know about the bus schedule right now, because it will not help me get out of the way of the bus.

Key Vulnerabilities– These are the elements that may contribute to making this situation a crisis. This list includes items that may or may not be directly related to the problem at hand. An example of something directly related could be that you had the same problem the previous year and thought you had fixed it. Something not directly related would be that contract negotiations with a labor union are about to start. While not directly related, the union may try to use the developing situation to make the company look bad.

Stakeholders– These are the individuals or groups who likely will have an interest in the situation and its outcome. The list includes internal and external parties. Especially for a complex situation, this list will be used to create a spreadsheet of communications assignments. The spreadsheet will list the stakeholders, those who will be accountable for communicating with each of them, as well as when to make the contacts and how, such as telephone, email, or formal letter.

Time Drivers– Timing matters during a crisis. With the initial surge of adrenaline, there often is an urge to start talking about the problem. It is crucial that the team understands clearly what the time constraints are. For example, when are the shipments of defective materials going to arrive at customer locations? In some crises there are regulatory requirements for reporting details to the government. Certain reporting deadlines can be very short. A few time drivers may not be directly related to the crisis but could impact the situation anyway. Perhaps a senior leader from your company is to meet with a government official in two days and will be in an awkward position whether she talks about the crisis situation or not.

 "We were so busy at the beginning that we had to put off our usual procrastination."

—Stu Poore, Crisis Production Leader, Gudenuff Technology

10.5 Half of What You Know is Wrong

An early mentor of mine at DuPont told me that at the outset of a crisis, "Half of what you know is wrong; you just don't know which half." How right he was! Even facts that seem straightforward and uncomplicated can prove to be in error later. With a torrent of information rushing at you, it is vital to separate facts from misinformation, from opinion, and from speculation.

 WAR STORY | **Your Initial Understanding Can Be Derailed**

One Christmas Eve, I got a call informing me that five railcars had gone off the tracks just outside a DuPont facility. Four contained chlorine and one contained propane. Although there were no known leaks, we obviously had a significant problem that needed immediate attention. On a later phone call, I learned that, in fact, nine rail cars had derailed. Nine. Railcars are large, and derailment is not a maybe-yes-maybe-no circumstance. Either the cars are on the tracks or they're not. Nine is not a large number of objects to count. For some reason though, the initial tally was in error.

Product-quality issues tend to be especially problematic in regard to getting the facts straight. It seems that each time you think you have a grip on the products involved and where they went, new information presents itself.

"The early information only added to the void of knowledge."
—Stu Poore, Crisis Production Leader, Gudenuff Technology

Numerous problems can arise when information is inaccurate, but two are the most troublesome. The first occurs when you start solving either the wrong problem or an incomplete version of the problem. The second is manifest when you start communicating one set of facts only to find out that you need to issue corrections, and your credibility is undermined.

To address the phenomenon of misinformation:

✱ Simply be aware that inaccurate information is common at the outset of a crisis. Do not be shocked; be prepared to adapt.

✱ Ask questions of those reporting on the situation. Inquire how they know what they're reporting is true and how the information can be further verified. This step is especially important for the most crucial aspects of the situation. For example, if you are issuing a product recall, you want to know that you are accurately describing the extent of the problem. You do not want to keep expanding the scope of the recall.

Key Point: The Fog of War

☑ During battle, as increasing amounts of information become available, combat leaders can find themselves less and less certain of their circumstance and capabilities. The fog of facts and figures often inhibits understanding and strategic decisions.

11

Structuring for Efficiency and Effectiveness

What's In This Chapter:

11.1 Situation Leader and Senior Sponsors

"Who's in charge here?" sounds like a simple and basic question, and it is. Unfortunately, it often stumps a crisis team, even one whose members have been working together for a while.

During my career, I was sent in many times to help a team that had been struggling to deal with a difficult situation. Frequently, it is not only the complexity of the situation that trips up a team, it is also that they have failed to get some basic elements in place for their crisis response. The most basic and important element: Choosing the right team leader.

Key Point:

☑ If you are building a house and do not get the foundation laid square, you will forever be struggling to make the rest of the structure line up.

 WAR STORY | **Choosing the Right Leader**

Immediately after the earthquake, tsunami, and Fukushima nuclear plant disaster in Japan, DuPont faced challenges due to damaged facilities and disrupted supply chains. The problems were compounded by a lack of good information about the health threats of the emerging radiation situation.

We quickly established a team, but it was not readily apparent who should be in charge. Although I was the global crisis leader, I knew that we needed to consider others who, given the special circumstances on the other side of the world, would be better suited to take the helm. We had a new crisis leader for the Asia-Pacific Region, bright and technically competent—but untested. We had the president of DuPont-Japan, a capable leader who had earned the trust of the DuPont-Japan employees—but who had family members missing in the wake of the tsunami. Eventually, his family members were found to be safe, but the initial uncertainty added to the stress that was felt by all of the employees and their families. Finally, an American who was living in Tokyo and serving as president of DuPont East Asia, an intelligent business leader with excellent people skills and a good appreciation for the Japanese culture, rose to take the reins. The important point was to be clear who actually was in charge.

I have learned not to step into an unfolding situation and bluntly ask, "Who's in charge here?" because the question can create embarrassment and awkwardness: embarrassment if the team hasn't defined who the leader is; awkwardness when there are two, three, or more people who feel they should be the leader. When I helped teams work through the process of determining the team leader, often the decision was made outside the meeting room lest it create added tension. Sometimes the boss overseeing the entire business was the best person to make the call.

I use the term "Situation Leader" as the designation for the person who is hands-on leading the team. So, you ask, what happened to the term "Crisis Leader?" It has been used a number of times earlier. I have learned not to call the leader of the response team the "Crisis Leader" for two reasons. One is that the team quickly can descend into a debate over whether the situation really is a crisis. A semantic debate adds no value and wastes precious time. The other problem with the term "Crisis Leader" is more serious and more complicated: if you get into litigation, plaintiffs' attorneys may raise the notion that because there was a crisis manager, the situation was, in fact, a crisis—implying an out-of-control disaster. The word "crisis" carries baggage with it. Use it with caution.

The situation leader is the person who owns the major decisions. For example, if you have a product-quality issue, the product manager should be the situation leader. Think of it this way: if the team decides a recall is warranted, the product manager needs to be directly involved in that decision.

The Situation Leader:

• owns the major decisions.
• updates senior-level sponsors on a regular and formal basis.

The Process Leader:

• directs how the team will operate
• facilitates team meetings

In the most intense situations, there will be one or more people higher up in the organization who also will want and need to have a major oversight role. Establish those individuals as the "Sponsors" or use some other such term that works for your organization. The situation leader updates the sponsors on a regular and formal basis. The sponsors are responsible for resources, policy decisions, and ensuring that the team understands the bigger picture regarding the impacts and outcomes of what they are deciding and doing.

Key Point:

☑ To create a structure that works in your culture, make it clear who is in charge and ensure visible support from upper levels of the management.

11.2 Process Leader

A major cause of a poorly handled crisis often is that it is managed too narrowly. The most effective structure of a crisis team calls for broader team management wherein one of the leaders serves solely as the process facilitator with responsibility for directing how the team will operate and focusing on the myriad details of running the meetings. The business leader who is serving as the situation leader, then, is able to remain focused on the big picture, including key decisions. The business leader must be looking over the horizon at possible future developments and, in addition, be thinking about the larger implications for the company, its reputation, operations, and financial position.

If you have enough resources, assign someone to the role of process leader. Choose a person who:

* Will remain objective.

* Will remain calm in a tense room.

* Is a good facilitator who can lead the group in an orderly and efficient fashion.

* Is an effective listener.

* Can stay with the team for the long haul.

* Can draw on past crisis management experiences.

* Is a guardian against "groupthink" or against the bias created by a dominant personality.

When a crisis is complex, there may be several crisis teams working together to resolve different but related problems that demand different kinds of expertise. Someone must analyze the situation and orchestrate the procedure for determining and monitoring the course of action for all of the moving parts.

Ideally, the process leader is a crisis team manager separate from either the situation leader, the business leader, the financial leader, or any other person already wearing a different hat. A process leader who is not serving in any additional capacity on the crisis team ensures that the approach is objective and comprehensive.

Having an experienced process leader is important because a

good crisis response includes a holistic approach to all relevant aspects, which may include addressing customer needs, protecting the brand reputation, avoiding litigation, communicating with stakeholders, and managing costs. An objective process leader who is not invested in any of those crisis responses will foster a holistic assessment that not only takes in all dimensions of a situation, but also results in a comprehensive plan. And, as a somewhat independent party, the process leader also can try to mediate within the team should things become rocky from time to time.

With a separate person serving in this capacity—running the meetings and directing how the teams will operate—a business or product manager who is serving as the situation leader can gain crisis management experience and, at the same time, remain focused on the business implications.

Most facility managers or product managers, who are rising in the organization, do not have extensive crisis experience yet. It is easy to spot the senior leader who never gained that experience along the way and suddenly is handed a big problem to address. Novice errors become much more costly at the higher levels. Gaining that crisis management experience, therefore, is enormously valuable for one's career. But learning to be an effective crisis manager in the midst of a significant real-world crisis would be like trying to learn to be a professional firefighter by jumping into a major fire. A manager who has not previously dealt with a major crisis is best served when someone who has been there before guides the effort.

Key Point:

☑ Gaining experience in managing a crisis is enormously valuable for one's career.

Those who would become a competent process leader, must gain the following experience and abilities.

Skills– Nobody learns to swim while standing on the deck of the pool. The person being trained to lead the crisis process must practice many techniques, including being a good listener, which means "listening"—not just with the ears, but also with the eyes to pick up signals from body language.

Ability to weave across the workstreams– Catching the hidden patterns and trends of a discussion often means observing from a step back. The best options may lie in the gray areas. Shining a light on those spaces can add great value to the discussion for a team that is lost in its own fog of information.

Self-confidence– The process leader must be willing to jump into the middle of an ambiguous and uncertain situation, including when that means getting up in front of a room of stressed-out professionals to guide them, time and again, even though the path is unclear.

Ability to trust the team– The process leader must be able to frame the questions but should not try to answer them all. It can be difficult to put personal views and ego aside so that, by providing a framework for the team members, they will figure out the best ways to proceed. In the long run, though, solutions generated by the whole team tend to be better because they are more holistic. Moreover, the team more readily will implement a plan they developed.

Trust of senior leaders– The senior leadership team needs to trust that the process leader knows what he or she is doing. Crisis situations are high-stakes problems for the businesses and for the careers of the individuals involved. Trust is earned only by showing you can do it. And showing you can do it only comes from the experience of trying and learning by doing.

Key Point:

☑ The situation leader is the person who "hands-on" leads the team—the one who makes the major decisions and sees that they are efficiently and effectively carried out. The process leader, drawing on past experiences and instructing on best practices, runs the meetings and directs how the team will operate.

Think hard about who has the capacity and the interest to make crisis management their competency. Not everyone has the character "flaws" that will allow them to do this. At least once during each crisis I lead, I get the feeling of, "What the #%*@ am I doing up here?! A smart person would run away."

....

"A person who chooses a career in crisis management generally has a propensity to flee from safety."
—Paul Dice, Crisis Management Expert

....

11.3 Core Team

The Core Team is the hands-on group that does the work of managing the crisis. The Core Team should comprise one person from each key function, discipline, or group. For example, you might have one regulatory expert, one public affairs specialist, one lawyer, one technical expert, one HR person, one finance manager. Include only those who have a strategic role to play. If you don't need an IT person on the team, don't include one.

Key Point:
....

☑ Loading the Core Team with more than one representative from each discipline slows and complicates the functioning of the team.

....

For the sake of efficiency and effectiveness in guiding a crisis response, I have learned to hold the line and limit the Core Team to only one person from each area of expertise. When you pare down the group to the designated Core Team, however, you often end up with some hurt feelings: "Here we are, facing the biggest challenge to our business in a long time, and I am not one of the people chosen to work on it. There must be something wrong."

11.4 Critical People Resources

Beyond the Core Team is a ring of people to be viewed as expanded resources. It is helpful to call them the "Critical Resources" or some such name that describes the value they bring. For example, because "stuff happens," you need a designated alternate for each Core Team member. You want to know from the outset who will step in if someone gets sick or has a family emergency. The lead person for each role should regularly keep the alternate up to speed. Usually, the alternates are on the Critical Resources list for the work streams or sub-groups, so that they already will be immersed in the work should they be called up.

> *"Having a meeting with just some of the key people is like showing up at the Beatles' recording studio with just Ringo and George."*
> —*Michael Clarke, Senior Attorney*

It is important to list the names of the team members on the whiteboard in the team room. People want and need to see their names on the board so that when the boss is reviewing the team's work, they will get some credit. But also, by putting people's names on the Critical Resources list, you help deal with hurt feelings that may have developed when you announced who would be on the Core Team.

Do not just list the team members; draw a picture. Depicting the team as two concentric circles with spokes radiating outward helps people visualize how the team is constructed.

War Story | Drawing Two Circles in India

I once had to fly all the way to Hyderabad, India, to draw two circles. A crisis team had created confusion by listing the team members on a bewildering Excel spreadsheet. I wondered: Why Excel? Are they planning to add up all the phone numbers at the bottom of the page? Joking aside, when instead, we defined the team by drawing two concentric circles—the names in the inner circle labeled Core Team and the names in the surrounding circle labeled Critical Resources—people in each group not only could see who had what role, but the relationship of the central Core Team members and the Critical Resources members immediately became clear. Although I had much more to do on the trip than to draw two circles, defining the team was a foundation stone for the plan we created for dealing with a series of ongoing, destructive protests by a group opposed to a company project.

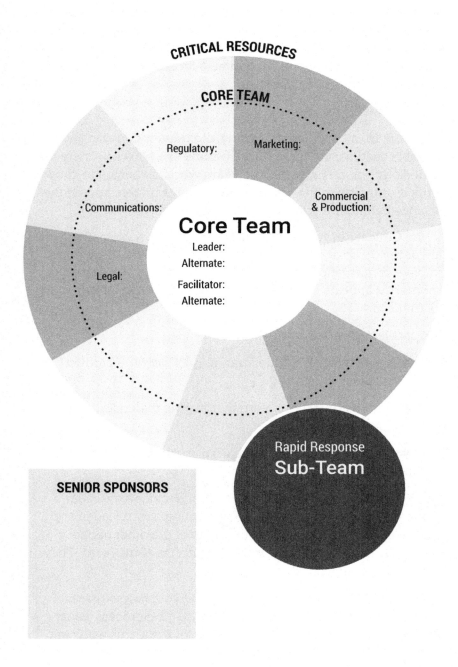

95

11.5 Workstreams

Workstreams are the areas of activity that feed into the overall project. For complex crisis situations, there are multiple workstreams running on parallel tracks. The Core Team member for each functional area is accountable for staying on top of the tasks being done in that arena.

Imagine this scenario:

You work for a cosmetics company and there is concern about possible bacterial contamination in some eye makeup. There is a toxicology person on your Core Team who is expected to know what is going on in the workstream aimed at understanding the science behind the concern.

In the Critical Resources circle there are other people named who are doing the toxicological research to get answers. They hope to have confirmation in the next 24 hours, but in the present moment it appears that you do have a problem and a recall must be initiated.

On parallel tracks you have:

✱ a supply-chain group arranging for how the product returns will be handled.

✱ a communications team drafting the materials that will announce the recall.

✱ a government relations team planning for notifications and interactions.

On the Core Team, then, in addition to the toxicology leader, you have a supply chain leader, a communications leader, and a government relations leader, but none of the other people contributing on those workstreams are on the Core Team. They are the Critical Resources.

If you are not careful, you quickly can get your workstreams operating outside of an efficient sequence. The process leader should furnish a timetable to govern when the teams will meet. In reality, there are many cross linkages among the workstreams, and effort is required to make sure they do not become entangled or inefficient. The next chapter provides specifics on how to sequence the workstream meetings for effective coordination.

"Never mistake motion for action."

—Ernest Hemingway

11.6 Managing Internal Expectations

A crisis of significance to the organization should have the attention of upper management. It is crucial to have the support of senior leaders for the work of the team. But because the top brass are not in every meeting, they will not be aware of all of the details. They also may have unrealistic expectations about how a situation will be resolved. Unrealistic expectations may lie on either side of reality. Some leaders may see the predicament as a much greater problem than it is likely to be. Others may be dismissive and assume the team is overreacting to a minor issue.

For most situations, no one will have a precise fix on how any given situation will turn out. You should, though, be able to plot a range of possible outcomes. Chapter 14, Section 4 explains use of the Pause & Reflect tool, which quickly lines out Best Case, Probable Case, and Worst Case scenarios. Primary use of the tool is to build offensive and defensive strategies and to assure proper resourcing. Secondary use is to show the three scenarios to senior leaders to help bracket their expectations. The Best Case scenario may not be all that good, and it's important for them to understand that. On the other hand, the Worst Case scenario may not be as terrible as they were imagining.

The Pause & Reflect tool can be updated periodically during an evolving crisis. Each time, the results can be shared with senior management to help recalibrate their understanding of projected future outcomes.

Regardless whether the expectations of senior leaders are managed with a formal process like the Pause & Reflect tool or with a less formal approach, the situation leader should regularly discuss expectations with the bosses so they recognize what the future may hold.

11.7 Buffering Senior Leaders

While the CEO should remain appropriately aware of any serious problem facing the company, that involvement should be measured and appropriate to the problem. There are times when a CEO might want to be at arm's length from the management of the crisis, times when it might even be a liability for the CEO to know lots of details and to be a hands-on player.

It may be time for the CEO to be at arm's length:

> ✱ When a crisis is becoming a black hole that pulls everyone's time and attention into its vortex. One of the challenges of the CEO during a crisis is to make sure the company continues to function normally to the greatest extent possible.

> ✱ When another senior leader is more qualified. If the crisis is primarily of a financial nature, for example, the CFO may be the right person to represent senior management.

> ✱ When managing the crisis—a vital experience for a leader—is an opportunity for a rising star to gain real-world knowledge of the challenges of crisis management. Upper management then can watch the potential future senior leader deal with the stress, ambiguity, and pressure of a crisis.

Whatever the reason for buffering the CEO and other top management, it should be clear who actually is representing them in directing the company's response. Too many cooks most certainly will spoil the broth. Moreover, if the CEO is not personally engaged, it should be explicitly stated who is going to keep the upper level appropriately informed.

11.8 The Hourglass Function

In an hourglass, the sand flows steadily through the narrow neck between the large bulb at the top and the similar bulb below. For a high-visibility, rapidly evolving crisis, you may need to set up an hourglass function for the flow of information.

Designate one person as the central point through which all information will funnel. The purpose is to have one person who always has the full and up-to-date view of what is happening. This task could be assigned to a Public Affairs specialist. Train everyone to understand that all new information must go to the person in the hourglass role first. That person, then, to satisfy the great thirst for information during the rapidly evolving crisis, will put out regular communications to those with a need to know. Alternatively, in situations where written communications may be ill-advised due to the lack of available facts, holding periodic briefings may meet the need.

Regardless of the situation, without an organized information collection and distribution system, two problems rapidly arise:

1. Rumors proliferate. It quickly becomes difficult to separate fact from rumor because both become entangled, recast, and repeated endlessly. The team then spends an inordinate amount of time chasing false leads and correcting inaccuracies.

2. No one has a complete view at any one time. Just as in the Indian parable of the blind men and the elephant, some people may have an accurate assessment of portions of the situation, but no one has the full view.

How you collect and disseminate information is tricky during a crisis, especially one that has the potential for litigation. Moreover, failure to set up such a system can have its own set of risks.

Work with your attorney to assess how best to approach the challenges. You will know you have the wrong attorney if, after obtaining legal input, you have nothing useful to communicate. Not communicating can send a strong message, but it may not be what you intended.

Key Point:

☑ Saying nothing often communicates a great deal, but it may not be what you intended.

CHAPTER

12

Setting the Pace for Effective Management

What's In This Chapter:

12.1 Structured Meetings for Effective Management

Meetings that take place in a business or an organization sometimes are viewed as a necessary evil. But when a crisis strikes, well-run meetings are the key to effective response. To ensure efficiency and effectiveness, team meetings should:

* Be scheduled as soon as a crisis begins.

* Start on time.

* Last no more than an hour if at all possible.

* Be run in a disciplined, focused way.

* Take place in a secure, well-supplied room set up as a crisis center.

✱ Be led by the Situation Leader or the Process Leader.

✱ Follow an agreed-upon agenda.

✱ Make use of tools and techniques known to aid organization and follow up.

✱ End on time.

12.2 Setup for Successful Team Meetings

Create and communicate a meeting schedule— The process leader should create an overall calendar of team meetings. As soon as the need to have multiple team meetings seems likely, get the meeting dates on the calendars of the team members. It is far easier to cancel a meeting than to find a slot at the last minute that suits everyone.

Holding Core Team meetings at noon helps in a number of ways. If you have a budget to buy pizza or sandwiches for the group, you ensure that they will show up for the meeting and more important, you make sure they are getting something to eat. In the press of a crisis, it is far too easy to skip meals. That is unhealthy and counterproductive. People who skip meals become cranky and sluggish. Everyone should police the team in this regard, even if it's a bring your own. The leaders should set the model and encourage others to eat regularly as well.

In a fast-breaking or rapidly changing crisis, the Core Team may need to have more than one meeting a day: the start and the end of the day can work well. You then can sequence your workstream meetings in the middle of the day. The important point is to set regular times so that team members can plan the rest of their days around them.

Start on time / End on time— Because time is precious in crisis management, the team leader must demonstrate the expectation that everyone will attend all scheduled meetings, will be there on time, and will be ready to go. If, in the initial phase of the crisis, meetings do not start on time, some team members quickly feel at liberty to wander in late. Soon time is going to waste because folks who are on time end up sitting for 15, 20, or even 30 minutes just waiting for the meeting to begin. You simply cannot afford that waste.

Each meeting, then—whether it is a sub-group meeting to focus on workstream efforts, the Core Team daily meeting, or the sponsor-group reviews—must be conducted with great efficiency and discipline. With an agenda that gives structure to the meeting, an experienced meeting facilitator will maintain focus on what is urgent and of greatest importance and will stem discussion and work that should be handled offline. Even in complex situations, team members must meet on time, get through the agenda, and then adjourn in order to get on with the offline crisis work as well as their regular jobs.

Stick to a one-hour limit— With rare exceptions, no meeting should run longer than one hour. If meetings routinely run longer, something is wrong. Most likely it is one of the following:

The process leader is allowing one or more people to talk too long.

The team is working on issues during the meeting that would be better handled by a sub-group outside the room; only the results of the sub-group work need to be reported at the meeting. Be alert for times when the whole team is trying to solve a problem that really is the work of one subset of the team.

The wrong people are involved if they cannot discern the difference between imparting information crucial to the overall success of managing the crisis at hand versus rambling on about their specific activities and the individual problems they face.

The leader is not injecting the discipline needed to start and stop the meetings on time.

"Our crisis team works so hard that once it goes into the crisis room it never comes back out."

—Stu Poore, Crisis Production Leader, Gudenuff Technology

Run disciplined, focused meetings— Workstream sub-groups should sequence their meetings in order to mesh efficiently and effectively. In reality, there are many cross linkages among the workstreams, so it is vital that they strive for good coordination.

The following is a useful daily sequence if you have multiple workstreams and everyone is in the same time zone:

Early morning– Each workstream sub-group

> ✱ Meets to line out its work and the progress it is making.
>
> ✱ Highlights critical unknowns and resource gaps.
>
> ✱ Drafts recommendations for current items that need to be considered by the Core Team. This step is especially important.

Noon– **The Core Team**

> ✱ Meets with each workstream leader reporting on that sub-group's work.
>
> ✱ Makes decisions on recommendations from the workstream sub-groups.
>
> ✱ Addresses resource needs and critical decisions on an ongoing basis.

Late in the day– **The Situation Leader**

> ✱ Meets with the Senior Sponsor(s) to provide an update on progress, as well as on gaps in the understanding of the situation.
>
> ✱ Brings up any items that need to be considered higher up in the organization.

If you are working across time zones, coordination of team meetings becomes a bit more complicated, but the concepts and general sequencing are the same.

 War Story | **Hurricanes Katrina and Rita**

During hurricanes Katrina and Rita, fourteen DuPont facilities along the Gulf Coast were affected to varying degrees. In the mornings, all workstream sub-groups had their own team meetings, which fed into a noon conference call with the Core Team. The Core Team leader, then, was well versed to report to the senior leaders during the Corporate Crisis Management Committee meeting that was scheduled for mid-afternoon each day.

12.3 Agenda for the Initial Meeting

As a crisis develops, there is a great deal going on, both stated and unstated. Invariably, there is much angst in the room for reasons that are obvious and sometimes for reasons that are not so obvious. And there may be hidden agendas or secrets that are potentially problematic.

Chapter 10 discussed the psychology and sensitivities of the first meeting when the crisis team assembles, and some tools were described for gathering the most important information. This section provides an annotated agenda for how to run that initial meeting, which likely will feel at least somewhat tense and chaotic. People having "just heard about it" will come in late. There also may be some speculation and whispering: "What happened?" "Why is he or she here?"

Creating order with an agenda written on the whiteboard or on a flip chart will help calm people down. The agenda shows folks that there is going to be a process for managing the situation.

Agenda for the Initial Meeting

1. Brief opening remarks by the senior person in the room

✱ The comments should clarify why the group is assembled and state the importance of having everyone pull together.

✱ If a situation leader has been decided upon, the beginning of the initial meeting is the right time for the boss to "anoint" him or her to ensure that everyone knows that the newly designated leader is in charge and has the support of upper management.

2. Agenda Review

✱ The process leader walks through the agenda written on the board. If there is no process leader yet, the situation leader or a delegate can do the walk-through.

✱ The person who presents the agenda is then in position as the person who will facilitate the meeting.

✱ The meeting facilitator should advise the group that the meeting will be kept to one hour—or whatever the allotted time is—and that everyone's cooperation is needed to remain on task with the agenda. Moreover, not everything will be solved immediately.

3. Records Management reminder

The need for good records management practices was noted in Chapter 10, Section 3. The topic should be covered at this point in the agenda. This is also a good time to emphasize the need for protecting the confidentiality of the discussions in the room.

4. Box Your Thoughts tool

The meeting facilitator:

✱ Draws columns on the whiteboard and explains the use of the tool. (See Chapter 10.)

✱ Creates an Action Items column on the whiteboard as well.

5. Situation Overview

The situation leader, or the person most qualified to describe the situation, gives an overview of the developing crisis. It is important that one person take the lead, lest the meeting descend into disarray with everyone chiming in at random.

After the situation has been reviewed by the most qualified person, others can be called on one-at-a-time to add to, clarify, or correct what has been said.

The meeting facilitator should advise the group that all of the information is not yet known and that no doubt the team will continue to clarify the understanding of the situation in the near future. Comments such as these help to "normalize" what may feel like confusion or ambiguity and thus help to calm people.

Quick questions for clarification should be answered. But questions such as "How could this have happened?" although important, often are not a good use of time at this stage. Place those questions on a list off to the side of a whiteboard; make a commitment to come back to them on another day. The meeting facilitator also must be alert for internal sniping. The team does not have time to waste with people trying to assign blame.

6. Roundtable Commentary

One person from each group represented should take the lead in providing a brief comment on what the situation could mean from their group's perspective. For example, the Public Affairs specialist could say: "This situation is highly likely to generate attention from traditional news media and social media." The PA specialist then commits to drafting a standby statement immediately. The Sales and Marketing person might say: "We will need to reach out to key customers ASAP." By eliciting a few brief comments from each group representative, the facilitator moves the discussion quickly around the room.

Throughout the situation overview and the roundtable commentary, the facilitator will have made notes in the Box Your Thoughts columns or as Action Items. Others in the room will have helped by listening to comments and then suggesting, for example, "That sounds like a Critical Unknown to me."

Once the group has been presented with the broad strokes of the overview and the roundtable commentary, the meeting facilitator states that because there is a serious problem to work on, it is urgent to organize quickly for action.

7. Steps for getting organized include:

✱ Establish a Core Team as discussed in Chapter 11, Section 3. Draw the concentric circles on the whiteboard and explain how the structure will work. Ask the group what key roles need to be represented by those on the Core Team and what Critical Resources may be required. If there are people who obviously should be named to the Core Team, list them. If some roles and assignments will require offline discussion, that is okay. You should list the need to fill in the remaining names for either the Core Team or Critical Resources on the team chart as an Action Item. This and all Action Items must include who has the assignment and when it will be completed.

✱ Establish a regular meeting schedule for the Core Team and set up the sequencing for other work to feed into that schedule.

✱ Make sure the overall effort is properly resourced. Do you have the right people and equipment to effectively address the situation? If there are gaps, create Action Items to fill them.

8. It is then time to review the columns from the Box Your Thoughts tool.

✱ If there are enough Positive Points to get started with a Core Statement, entertain a brief discussion and then assign offline work to the communications team. Note the assignment on the Action Item list.

✱ Determine which of the Critical Unknowns are most crucial and establish a process for deciding whether to go after relevant information. Also, consider what would happen next if answers that come back are not what you were hoping for?

✱ The group can discuss Key Vulnerabilities if time allows. At a minimum, you will need strategies for how to deal with the crucial vulnerabilities. The group should decide whether to launch into a session to begin developing those strategies or whether it would be better to start that work offline. If the choice is to begin offline, note that assignment on the Action Item list.

✱ The Stakeholders list will be used to target and time your communications.

✱ The Time Drivers, which ultimately determine the urgency of actions, will factor into much of what you do and how you do it.

9. Review the Action Items

Make sure each has a deadline and the name of the person accountable for completion.

10. Discuss any logistics that have not been covered

Do you have a good room in which the team can meet on an ongoing basis? Can the room be designated for sole use by this team for an extended period? Does it contain the materials and supplies you will need such as a good speakerphone system, whiteboards, markers and any other equipment?

11. Adjourn the meeting with a sincere thank you

Ideally, this should be expressed by the senior leader. Remind the group that from that point forward, the Core Team will consist of the people named in the inside circle on the whiteboard and that other Critical Resources will be tapped to help drive various workstreams.

12.4 Agenda for Ongoing Team Meetings

By kicking off the process as described in the section above, you will have set the stage for how all future meetings will run. Note that what is described below for the Core Team also can be used for any sub-group meetings. It is equally important that those meetings be run with good discipline. Again, time is a precious commodity when a crisis befalls your organization. A routine meeting should not last longer than one hour. Efficiency matters.

Agenda for Core Team Meetings

1. Situation Update

The situation leader or a delegate will provide a brief update of what has happened since the previous team meeting.

2. Roundtable Updates

A brief update is provided for each of the roles represented on the Core Team. The representative for each function should talk about developments in their arena and any progress on their Action Items. As a guide, ask each sub-group or role representative to report briefly on:

* Progress on current activities

* Issues that have arisen

* Upcoming actions

* Barriers or concerns

For example, the Public Affairs specialist may provide a quick analysis of recent interactions with the news media and what the Public Affairs sub-group is doing to monitor and analyze social media posts. The PA specialist may highlight shortcomings in the existing talking points where they are inadequate to handle a rising area of interest. That does not mean that the whole Core Team does a deep dive into working up new answers. That work is done offline, including, as needed, any content input from the appropriate people. The new draft of the communications material is then run through the regular approval process.

As the meetings progress over time, some people may pass if they have nothing new to report. That is perfectly okay.

3. Group Decisions

Not everybody needs to work on or even comment on everything. The Core Team should allow most of the work to be done offline with recommendations brought in for approval. If those recommendations have not been covered in the Roundtable Updates, now is the time for those items to be discussed. Also, topics that merit the holistic attention of the Core Team can be debated at this point.

4. Rumors and Horizon Issues

The Core Team should make space on a regular basis for people to bring up longer term or broader issues as well as rumors or other topics that a team member believes warrant awareness of the group.

5. Action Item Review

The process leader goes over the Action Item list to make sure everything has been covered. This discipline lets everyone know that if they committed to do something, there is an expectation that it will get done.

6. Reminder about the Next Meeting

Make sure to have all meetings scheduled for the foreseeable need.

12.5 Use of Humor

Crisis management, by definition, is a tension-filled experience. Especially for those for whom it is their first opportunity to stare at a major problem with a range of solutions that goes from bad to worse to horrendous, it is natural to feel the strain from many angles. When you are worried about your business failing, fretting about the high profile of a big mistake, panicking about your workload, or wondering whether you are going to lose your job, stress feels like it is everywhere. The ugly specters that haunt your days only grow larger at night. It's hard to sleep when a crisis shares the pillow. The lack of sleep, in turn, compounds the problems of the day.

Humor can help to defuse a bit of the tension, but only if used carefully. Some may see use of humor as evidence that you are not taking a dire situation seriously. Others may see even a little levity as a distraction and a time waster.

Key Point:

☑ Using humor during a crisis is a risk. For a leader, self-deprecating humor may be the safest bet. Keep it light and quick.

 War Story | **A Bad Use of Humor**

My team and I had been dealing with a crisis for many weeks. One of our colleagues came into a Monday meeting griping about his truly enormous workload. He went on to complain that the past weekend was the end of grouse season, and he had only been able to get out hunting once during the entire year. I replied, "End of grouse season, huh? Does that mean you'll stop grousing now?" Bad shot on my part. If looks could kill, I'd be dead.

Some additional guidelines:

❋ Never target any individual other than yourself with even the slightest jab. Remember that everyone is under stress, even if they are not necessarily showing the effects. On a good day, a person may like the banter, but a crisis day is not a good day, and nerves can be near the surface.

✱ Test the waters with a toe. Throw out a little humorous line, preferably having thought it through in advance so that you have a chance to consider it a bit. See how it goes. If it flops, be prepared to quickly and sincerely apologize: "You know what, I should not have said that. My apologies. Let's get back on track."

✱ If you have trouble with the bunny slope at a ski resort on a sunny day, stay off the double-black-diamond trails during a blizzard. The same consideration holds true for using humor: If you are not normally good at telling a joke in a relaxed social setting, do not try it during a crisis.

✱ Humor on paper or in email is a bad idea and should not be used in writing under any circumstances. Emails and other written communications have no tone of voice. Even if you add a smiley face, your idea of a little joke can be ill-received. Even worse, what was intended as hyperbole or irony or "gallows humor" can come back to haunt you in the harsh light of a courtroom. A clever pun or a funny name for an adversary can bite the originator in a deposition or on a witness stand. "Clearly, Ms. Walker, you found this situation to be funny, didn't you? Well, I can assure you that the pain and suffering caused by use of defective products manufactured by your company was not at all humorous to my client."

 WAR STORY | **To Doodle, Or Not To Doodle**

To underscore the risks of documenting your feelings, consider the guy who drew a doodle of Humpty Dumpty sitting on a wall and then falling off. It was a mindless depiction of the hassles customers were encountering. How does it look, though, when those doodles are later presented during a deposition? They can be hard to explain under the pointed questions of a plaintiff's attorney.

12.6 Use of "War Stories"

My extensive experience in dealing with crises provided me with a vast reservoir of war stories. I used them somewhat frequently, but judiciously, when leading a crisis team.

Near the start of a crisis response, when getting to know a team, I often shared a brief tale of another situation. I always picked one I was sure they never had heard. "Just like you never heard of that situation," I would say to them, "the overwhelming majority of people in the company most likely never will hear of your situation either." As they descended into the hot and frightening fires of a crisis, feeling that the whole world was about to know about their screwed-up situation, I wanted them to know that they would get through it, and most people never would know it happened.

Telling a war story or two also told them something about me. I was often new to them and was arriving at a point in their careers when they looked their worst. In addition, I was from "corporate," which carries some baggage in any organization. I wanted them to be aware that I had experience that could be of particular value to them and, in addition, that similar problems occurred more often than they knew. Sometimes I said it aloud and sometimes I just implied it, but the message was that if we all worked together, we'd get through it. I knew people did not want to air their dirty laundry with a stranger from corporate, but I did my best to make them comfortable enough to work with me.

 War Story | **Truth or Consequences**

I tried hard to make Core Team meetings a safe place for people to put all the cards on the table. Sometimes, though, I would sense a person was holding back some information. At a break, I would chat casually with those people. I did so during one product-quality issue when I had a sense that one of the technical experts was not being entirely forthcoming.

When we walked down the hall to get a cup of coffee, I tried to assure him that if we would all just trust each other and work openly, we'd do fine. As it turned out, he actually was hiding some key information that would markedly change how we understood what we were dealing with. Unfortunately, he continued to hide the information until eventually it was discovered without his help. Mistakes are one thing, but concealment and cover-ups are another. He lost his job.

12.7 Avoiding the Martyr Syndrome

Most companies operate with lean staffing, even during normal periods. No one is sitting around with too little to do. That is especially true of the really good people, who happen to be the ones you want on a crisis team. Working on a crisis is an added burden. Everyone on the crisis team is carrying more than they normally do, and, frankly, more than they should.

While a heavy workload is the norm for many team members, the team leaders must be on the alert for martyrs. Those people load themselves up with work and then spend significant amounts of time making sure everyone knows how overloaded they are. One colleague, who was, in fact, very good at issues and crisis management and who generally did carry a heavy workload, was famous for the amount of time he wasted telling anyone who would listen how he did not have enough time to get everything done.

Another problem with martyrs is that often they do not know when to stop. Their lives are out of balance, and they do little on their own to correct that. Their families suffer, their health is neglected, and ultimately their work deteriorates because nobody can carry on like that without diminishing returns. Moreover, their irritable attitude creates a negative undercurrent among other team members.

People can be driven to the martyr role by a number of factors that frequently travel with a crisis:

❋ There is a great deal of attention from upper management. Here is a chance to stand out as the hardest worker.

❋ Especially at the outset of a crisis, there is far too much to do, far too little time, and far too few people to help manage it. People are hustling around trying to carry their share of the load. Some people come to enjoy the adrenaline rush of rallying to fight the fire, but then get addicted to it, creating their own sub-crises when the original one no longer provides the fix they need.

❋ Some people gripe about all the work they have to do every day anyway. The crisis gives them fresh grist for their mill.

❋ People perceive that everyone else is sacrificing, and they genuinely want to do their share out of fairness and loyalty to the team.

Through all of this, it can be hard to sort out the real problems from the background noise. As opposed to the Eeyore personality who is vocally in "woe is me" mode most days, my observation is that there are some workers who never complain at all but, in fact, are shouldering an ungodly share of the work. Leaders must protect these folks from themselves. Force them to take a break, and provide backup support.

Certainly we appreciate the heroic measures of all personnel during a crisis, but some behaviors can have a downside, both for the individual and for the team. Smart managers keep a close eye on behavior that might be crossing the line from productive to harmful. They then must address it, even if the person objects.

CHAPTER

13

Getting the Word Out

What's In This Chapter:

13.1 Choosing a Company Spokesperson

When a crisis strikes, selecting the right person to serve as the spokesperson is an important decision with many factors influencing the choice. First, you need to match the level of the person to the seriousness of the situation. If your crisis is a high-profile catastrophe that is going to drag the company name through the mud and cut the stock price by half, your spokesperson needs to be a senior leader, maybe even the CEO. On the other hand, if a serious problem primarily affects the local community around one of your facilities, your facility manager is more likely to be the right person. If the problem involves a specialized arena like engineering, accounting, or toxicology, you may want to think about a person with a matching background.

After determining the right individual to serve as the spokesperson, you need to make sure the person has been media trained. Beyond that you need to ask whether he or she has real-world experience in dealing with the press. You do not throw a novice to the wolves in a high profile controversy.

You also want to make sure that the person can relate to concerned stakeholders. It is generally a good idea to have your spokesperson be a native speaker of the language of the most interested stakeholders.

In addition to the basics described above, you need someone who will come across well. This is especially true if television or other visual media are involved. People take a cue from the appearance of the person and how the person responds to questions. There are many subtleties and nonverbal signals that are transmitted when a person speaks. Annoying habits can be a related issue. The person who injects "you know" into every sentence comes across poorly.

Key Point:

☑ Your spokesperson must exhibit caring, compassion, confidence, and competence.

 WAR STORY | **Conveying the Wrong Message**

A plant manager at a large DuPont facility was a caring and competent person who had an unfortunate habit of shrugging and chuckling when he got nervous. At a public meeting, when asked about risks to children from a proposed project, he shrugged and chuckled lightly. To the people in the audience, he conveyed that children's health was not a big deal to him. That was exactly the opposite of what he really felt and what he tried to say, but the message people received was one of not caring.

13.2 Your First Statement Out

In the lightning-fast world of social media and even for the somewhat slower traditional media, you must have a statement quickly ready for use in order to make the first news cycle. The longer the news stories say your company is unavailable for comment, the worse it will look, and the more others will fill the void of information.

Unfortunately, in the earliest phase of a crisis, facts are hard to come by. Moreover, the attorneys, in particular, instinctively will guide the team to avoid any comment based on less than a complete understanding of all of the facts, which often means not giving any comment at all. Going down that path is almost always a mistake.

 "At the outset of the crisis there were many more opinions than facts, so we went with the opinions."
—Stu Poore, Crisis Production Leader, Gudenuff Technology

To compound the situation, in the earliest phase of a crisis, the team often has not yet established a review and approval process for public statements. Lacking a defined process, a common default approach is to choose the safest route and include everyone. Thus, your first communication could have a gestation period of days rather than minutes or hours. You cannot allow the lack of an efficient approval process to prevent any comment from being made.

Key Point:

☑ Your initial statement can be as simple as "We're aware, and we care."

In order to get a statement out the door, be satisfied with something basic that everyone can agree on. "We're aware, and we care" is a good example. "We are aware of reports that [fill in a basic description of what is being alleged or reported]. We are concerned that our company [or product] is being implicated in the reports. We are investigating the situation to determine the facts and will provide more information when facts are known." If the attorney or another gatekeeper on the team cannot approve even such a simple statement, replace that individual on the team. That person will continue to cause problems that will only compound as you try to move forward.

CASE STUDY | Air Ambulance Crash in Nevada

In late 2016, four people were killed when a medevac air ambulance crashed in Nevada. The company that owned the aircraft quickly released a statement stating the few facts they had confirmed, and then added: "We are devastated by this event and wish we had answers to the many questions being asked at this time. We are cooperating fully with the National Transportation Safety Board and the Federal Aviation Administration as they investigate the accident."

With this brief statement, the company expressed its sorrow, stated what it knew to be true, acknowledged that it lacked additional facts at this time, and confirmed it would cooperate with government authorities. The company engaged swiftly and effectively as it addressed a tragic situation.

Key Point:

☑ Anything you say can and will be used against you in a court of law. Anything you are perceived to be hiding can and will be used against you in the court of public opinion—and perhaps also in a court of law. You must find something you can say and move forward quickly.

13.3 Connecting Your Statements to Your Core Values

The importance of Core Values in crisis management already has been discussed. Your public statement is one place where that is particularly true. Your Core Values can provide a secure foundation for your statements. If your Core Values are real—they cannot be window-dressing or words not backed up by your behavior—they can serve to anchor your statements. Nowhere is this more valid than with the statements that are most difficult to write perhaps due to a lack of good information or simply an embarrassing mistake that led to a disaster. Also, for a crisis that will be of long duration, tying your statements to your Core Values will help maintain continuity over the course of the crisis. People will see a consistent theme and will recognize that even though you are struggling with the complexity of the situation, you are guided by higher principles.

Key Point:

☑ Especially for the statements that are most difficult to write, your Core Values can serve as a firm foundation. If your Core Values are real, your statements will be true and reasonably connected to something solid and valid.

13.4 Core Statement

During most crises, you will need multiple communications that are tailored for the many stakeholders. You may want a letter to customers, an email to employees, a formal notification for government officials, and other targeted communications. You will get in trouble in multiple ways if you attempt to create separate documents for each need. You will waste a great deal of time, and you will struggle as you get tangled up trying to be consistent. A Core Statement provides a common description of the situation and your actions. From that statement, all communications can be tailored while remaining aligned.

Key Point:

☑ A Core Statement is your current description of the situation. This one statement serves as the basis for all of your communications, regardless of the targeted stakeholder.

To simplify and standardize your communications, draft one Core Statement that describes the situation and includes your position. Use that statement as the core for all other communications. Often a simple introductory paragraph and closing are all that are needed to tailor the communication to a specific audience. At other times, more detail must be added. For example, a letter to customers might have more information on alternatives you are suggesting or the expected timing of product delivery. That information would be added to the Core Statement in the letter.

Key Point:

☑ What you communicate inside the organization must be consistent with what you communicate to the outside world. Any asymmetry may be used against you.

Your Core Statement is dynamic, not static. It is updated as often as necessary, based on the emerging situation. For that reason, each statement should be clearly labeled with the date and even the time for a fast moving crisis.

In a crisis that is largely playing out through social media, your Core Statement may be described better as Core Content. It may, in fact, end up as a video message that relies heavily on visual depictions of the situation.

13.5 High, Medium, or Low Speak

Many topics become increasingly technical when you delve into the details. A medical crisis, an automotive-part recall, or a food contamination issue all can lead to highly technical levels of discussion. The question often arises: "What level of technical details should we include in our communications?" The answer depends on your audience.

One effective approach for meeting the needs of your audience is to consider their level of technical knowledge on the topic and then design communications to meet those needs and that level of understanding. Three technical levels may be helpful as you work to address multiple needs:

Highly technical– These communications are for the people with the most sophisticated knowledge in the field. Your communications can be at the ultimate degree of complexity in order to explain the topic, even reaching the level that might appear in a professional, peer-reviewed journal. Provide the information that top experts need to fully comprehend the situation.

Mid-level– These communications are for people who work in the field on a regular basis but do not necessarily have a Ph.D. in the scientific discipline. Certain regulatory officials, customers, and some reporters operate at this level. They can handle technical detail and understand the basic jargon of the industry, but they do not need or want the highly technical underpinnings.

Lay people– The vast majority of people will not comprehend the technical aspects. To satisfy the need for information in easily understood formats, provide some explanation of terms and concepts along the way.

To illustrate the three levels of technicality, imagine that you are managing a contamination problem in ground meat. You want to explain to various stakeholders the basic system you already have in place to check for contaminants and other problems. The mid-level person described above—perhaps a regulatory official with the Department of Agriculture—will know exactly what you mean when you reference your HACCP system. For the lay person, however, you will need to explain that HACCP stands for Hazard Analysis and Critical Control Points, and that HACCP is used in the food industry to identify potential food safety hazards so that key actions can be taken to reduce or eliminate the risk of the hazards being addressed. You might add that this mandatory system provides a rigorous framework for preventing problems and assessing issues. The highly technical folks, perhaps toxicologists working in the fast food industry, may want to see the data regarding the contaminant levels at a particular stage in your meat processing.

You always run the risk of missing the mark with your communications. The Goldilocks principle does not apply here; there is no "just right" level. The technical experts might feel you are denying them the opportunity to fully assess the situation and reach their own conclusions if you do not provide all the data behind your statements. On the other hand, the average citizen may think you are trying to snow them with a blizzard of data that they do not understand. A way around the dilemma is to give general access by nesting all of the pertinent information on your website. A well-designed website not only will allow people to pick the level of detail they want, but it also will make it easy to move readily from one level to another as needed.

⚠ Pitfall – *Putting ordinary terms in quotation marks often conveys that there is a gap between what you are writing and the real truth.*

13.6 Ask: What is Our Narrative?

People often best remember information through stories. When the details of your saga are long forgotten, people can be left with a general impression as their recollection of your company and how it responded to the crisis.

It is helpful to periodically step back and ask, "What story are we conveying? What is our narrative?" That is not to say you are "creating a story," as in trying to weave a false tale or spin the truth. The narrative should be the consistent theme that others will see if they step back from the situation.

> **On the struggle between Tibet and China:**
> *"It's not whose army wins; it's whose story wins."*
> —Stefan Halpern

The introspection of asking such questions is a good way to check on the impressions you are leaving. Are you coming across as a company that is fumbling with the logistics of a recall, or are you conveying that you are a company that cares about its customers and the impacts your problem is having on them? Are you expressing greatest concern about future litigation or are you transmitting a consistent theme of compassion for the community?

During a long-running crisis, periodically question the image you are communicating to evaluate the continuity in your messages and whether the given impression is what you want to be leaving with people. Consistency of messages, based on your Core Values and backed up by your behavior, regarding ethics or caring for the environment will shine through. To constantly say you care about the environment and then act like all you care about is saving money will look like hypocrisy.

Key Point:

☑ Periodically ask yourselves about the impression you are conveying.

"We're much too smart to be arrogant."
—Stu Poore, Crisis Production Leader, Gudenuff Technology

13.7 Electronic Team Room

An electronic team room, such as a SharePoint site, provides a secure space for crisis team members to store checklists and contact lists, share communications materials, track progress, and manage the many moving parts of a crisis.

In a fast-moving crisis, team members will wonder at times whether they have the most current Core Statement and Question and Answer list. Setting up an electronic team room, with access restricted to approved people, solves those problems by allowing the team to grab the right documents when they need them. If you do not give team members an easy way to access the documents, they will resort to going to the Public Affairs specialist or someone else on the team to ask them to send the most current version. That is a waste of everyone's time.

Ironically, a similar challenge occurs in a slow-moving crisis. Some crises play out over months or even years, with long lag times between activities. In that circumstance, team members struggle to find the statement at all, let alone know whether it is current.

Key Point:

☑ Creating an electronic team room for a restricted set of people allows all team members ready access to your key documents. Keep the most current Core Statement and Q&A list in the team room.

You want messages to all stakeholders to be consistent so that what you say to government officials aligns with your communications to customers, employees and everyone else. But be watchful, because your approved communications sometimes can change multiple times even in just one day as you gather facts and make progress in resolving the situation.

Each time your Core Statement or Q&A is updated, send it to the team room and remove the earlier version. Note that you must adhere to any legal "hold" orders when you remove materials.

Key Point:

☑ Messages to all stakeholders must be consistent so that what you say to any one group aligns with your communications to everyone else.

It is crucial to assign clear responsibility for editing rights and approval authority for all official communications.

13.8 Making Nothing Happen

An early mentor of mine told me that when we are working on an issue or a crisis, our job is to make nothing happen. I have always remembered his wise counsel. When we do our best work in managing an issue or a crisis, few people ever know. Success is when the problem goes away with barely a ripple. You address the concern and move on.

Although it is tough to measure something that does not happen or is less bad than it might have been, I have sometimes been tempted to walk into the boss' office, hold up the New York Times, and say, "You ought to see the article that's not in here." That would be a way to highlight the fact that we have done a good job of resolving the problem. While I never have done that, I have at times told management to listen to the quiet. I point out that their people are doing their regular jobs and are not being sucked into the black hole of a crisis that is larger than it needed to be.

Key Point:

☑ When working on an issue or crisis, the ideal is often to make nothing happen.

Keeping the crisis rumor mill quiet can sometimes mean not talking about the situation at all outside the team. That challenge means crisis management work is not for everyone. If you are someone who needs your coworkers to know what a great job you have done or how often you get face time with the boss, you will find this work frustrating. To begin with, you must resist the temptation from the outset to talk about the situation. By definition, a crisis is interesting. It is out of the ordinary, and it has inherent drama. Also, because upper levels of management are paying attention to it, others want to be in the know.

Here's the rub: Talking about the problem is almost certain to create a buzz in the organization. Next, as the buzz is embellished, rumors proliferate. You now have additional risk and extra work as you seek to correct the misinformation that is flowing in the halls and perhaps beyond because someone couldn't resist the urge to tell all.

13.9 Getting onto the Forgotten Track

Quiz

✱ In March 1989, what company caused the big oil spill in Prince William Sound, Alaska?

✱ In early 1990, there was another big spill (an estimated 400,000 gallons of crude oil) in an environmentally sensitive spot near Huntington Beach in Southern California. In the highly charged media environment, there was lots of coverage. What company caused that spill?

✱ In 2010, from April through September, what oil company was a major player in the Deepwater Horizon oil spill in the Gulf of Mexico?

✱ In January 1988, what oil company caused a huge oil spill into the Monongahela River near Pittsburgh? The oil was carried by the Monongahela River into the Ohio River, temporarily contaminating drinking water sources for an estimated one million people in Pennsylvania, West Virginia, and Ohio, contaminating river ecosystems, killing wildlife, damaging private property, and adversely affecting businesses in the area. The situation generated enormous media coverage for a long period.

Answers: Exxon, BP, BP, Ashland

All of these situations were serious environmental problems. All of them triggered a great deal of media coverage and public concern. Chances are, though, that you had answers for just two of the four questions. If you got only answers 1 and 3 correct, you are in the vast majority. Why is it that some crises remain in our memories, becoming infamous cultural icons, while others fade away until only those people directly impacted remember them?

The major determining factor in whether a crisis endures in the public memory has much to do with how it was managed. If the general populace feels the company responsible for the crisis stepped up to own the problem, to design the solution, and then followed through to implement the solution, the memory will fade. If the company tried to point a finger at others and was perceived as mishandling the cleanup, the narrative shifts from being solely about what actually happened to being about corporate malfeasance, incompetence, and insensitivity.

In the BP spill at Huntington Beach, they stepped up and owned the problem. In the Ashland spill into the Monongahela River, the CEO went to the river's shoreline and said in essence, "We screwed up, and we will fix it." In such instances, the public gaze shifts away and the news media soon move on to something with greater tension and drama. People forget.

Key Point:

☑ The kind of response after an incident occurs helps to determine how and whether people remember what happened.

In the fall of 2011, it came to light that Pennsylvania State University appeared to be systematically covering up child sexual abuse by one of the assistant coaches in its storied football program. The allegations were horrendous and repulsive. The alleged offenses cried out for justice. But the university mismanaged the crisis at each turn. It is impossible to imagine that the Penn State board of trustees met to debate which side of the child abuse issue they should be on. Yet in the public eye they floundered and stumbled. They had forewarning that the alleged situation was going to burst into public view, yet they seemed totally unprepared when it actually did. Their lack of effective leadership and perceived lack of a moral compass (real-world Core Values) have now ensured that this esteemed and great university will bear a significant black mark for a very long time. People will not forget.

At a distance it can seem obvious what the right calls are. But inside the conference room, the choices do not always appear clear cut, and the decisions often can be gut-wrenching. Chapter 14, Section 3 provides detailed guidance on how to make decisions when all you have are bad options.

In the Core Values section of Chapter 6, there is a list of the DuPont Crisis Management Principles that mirrored the company's Core Values. One of the principles stated, "We will acknowledge appropriate responsibility immediately and determine liability after the facts are known." That does not mean the company is going to blindly raise its hand and claim responsibility for something that is not its fault. It does mean, though, that the company should seriously look at the bold move of stepping up when appropriate. Even when a company knows it is at fault, management often is reluctant to step forward because of what that will mean in regard to future litigation. The pitfall here is that if you define your objectives too narrowly, you may win on one front but actually lose on the larger goal of holistically protecting the company. You may permanently sacrifice your company's reputation because of your fear of litigation down the road.

....

⚠ Pitfall – *If you define your objectives too narrowly you may win on one front but actually lose on the larger goal of holistically protecting the company.*

....

Ironically, it may be harder to win in court in the years to come if the jury pool has a general memory of your behavior as trying to hide from the obvious. Their inclination may be to punish you further for not stepping up.

3.10 Legal vs. Ethical Quadrants

It is easy to slip into the trap of assuming that, because what you did was legal, it also was ethical. There is a difference between doing what you have a right to do and doing what is right.

⚠ *Pitfall – Do not assume that because what you are doing is legal, it is also ethical.*

 WAR STORY | **Water, Water, Everywhere...**

As a contractor to the EPA under the Superfund program, I was standing in a family's kitchen when we did a repeat sample of their drinking water to confirm that it was contaminated. From the first round of tests, we essentially knew that it was, but because we were working for the EPA, the law required that we not communicate the information until it was confirmed with a separate test. Unfortunately, due to a backlog of work in the approved laboratories, that confirmation would be months in coming. Standing there with a very pleasant mother and her cute child, how was I to answer when she asked trustingly whether it was safe to drink the water? I told her that we had concerns, and that was why we were back. I said that I, too, had a young child and that if it were me, I would get bottled water until the results came back. I very well may have broken the law by telling her that, but I feel strongly that what I did was ethically correct.

Legal vs. Ethical Quadrants

The ideal, of course, is to be in the upper right quadrant where you are doing what is both legally and ethically right. Conversely, if you find yourself in the lower left quadrant where what is being considered is both illegal and unethical, you need to report that state of affairs to management. If they do not act, you need to consider reporting the problem to external authorities. Moreover, if it is a serious situation where the well-being of people or the environment is at risk, you must tell someone outside the company. You have an ethical obligation to do something. Of course such a move may come with personal consequences. Courage and a good moral compass are needed.

The other two quadrants present difficult dilemmas. Is what is being proposed illegal but essentially the right thing to do? Or is the proposal a strictly legal approach but inadequate to the point of being unethical? These two quadrants require a sound approach to decision making. More important, they require team members who have good moral judgment and the courage to stand up for what is right even when doing so is likely to create additional problems or risks.

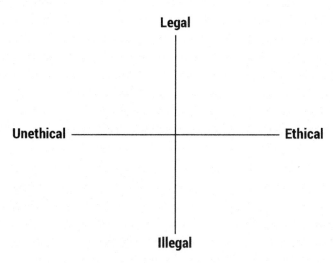

 WAR STORY | **He Punted**

Perhaps one of the saddest examples of someone who did what was legally required but was perceived as having fallen short in fulfilling his ethical obligation is Joe Paterno, legendary football coach at Penn State. When a graduate assistant told Coach Paterno he had seen inappropriate behavior between an assistant coach and a young boy in the shower, Paterno reported the abuse to his supervisors, but he did not publicly decry the actions of the coach and seek to have him fired. He did what the law required, but he was severely criticized and fired for not having done more.

Key Point:

- ☑ Doing what is right is always the best route. Sometimes figuring out what is right can be exceedingly difficult.

13.11 Expectation Management

Business issues often arise when there is a gap between an organization's behavior and stakeholder expectations. Crises can arise in turn from mismanagement of an issue. Into this gap fall many individuals and institutions. Bill Clinton, a smart and effective president, has a permanent stain on his reputation because his personal behavior did not meet public expectations, either regarding his unsavory conduct in the White House or in what he did after his behavior came to light.

Similarly, the Catholic Church failed terribly to meet public expectations. It was not bad enough that there was child abuse by clergy, but there is overwhelming evidence that the Church did not step up to the problem. Rather, some people in authority within the Church systematically covered up the problem for decades. Think of it this way—if there was a rogue motorcycle gang whose members were abusing children and the larger group covered it up, that would be an outrage. How much worse, then, to have a church do the same?

Companies often set their own standards of behavior. If you are running a used car dealership and you sell cars with undisclosed problems, that scam is framed differently than if you are Toyota, which prides itself on selling safe and reliable automobiles. When Toyota came under scrutiny for allegedly selling cars with defects, the company stumbled in managing the situation, thus severely damaging its reputation. Similarly, General Motors and Volkswagen both have fallen far short of public expectations. In 2014, GM finally owned up to the fact that for years it had been selling cars with dangerously faulty ignition switches. Late in 2015, VW was pressured into admitting it purposefully had marketed diesel cars with software designed to fool the emissions tests. Only after West Virginia University researchers discovered the situation and alerted the EPA did VW reluctantly come clean about what it had done. All three car companies have suffered severe financial and reputational damage.

Society also sets expectations. The public expects companies to act in ethical ways and to keep the greater good of society in view. The banking industry earned a big black eye in the financial crisis that exploded in 2008. The banks and other financial institutions were seen as greedy, conniving villains who cost many people and small businesses a great deal. Innocent people lost their homes and their livelihoods.

Many citizens hold a bias against large multinational corporations. MNCs are painted with a broad brush as being avaricious, uncaring, and only out for profits. When a crisis strikes, a large company often begins the response process lacking support of some members of the public simply because it is an MNC. In that case, public perceptions can cast a cloud of suspicion over everything the company says and does when responding to the crisis. Even as the firm is genuinely trying hard to address a negative situation, it will be swimming upstream trying to prove it is not as bad as people imagine.

CHAPTER

14

Making Tough Decisions

What's In This Chapter:

14.1 It's All About Decision-making

A crisis, by its very nature, is a situation in which you are faced with an acute problem and a range of undesirable options as solutions. You cannot stay where you are, and you cannot move without creating more problems. Despite too little time; a lack of adequate, valid information; and the glare of the public spotlight, you need to do something. How, under these pressing circumstances, do you make a "good" decision about which course of action to take?

"Crisis management really comes down to whether we can make good decisions quickly."
    —Chad Holliday, former CEO, DuPont

14.2 Objectives – What Exactly are We Trying to Do Here?

A crucial first step—and one often skipped—is to ask: What exactly are we trying to do here? Stated another way: What would success look like?

⚠ *Pitfall – Teams often skip asking what they are trying to accomplish, or they instinctively define success too narrowly. Most problematic is that team members may be operating with different definitions of success.*

The over-riding concern is not just that the team has failed to discuss what they are trying to accomplish, but that the various team members often have different concepts of what success looks like and how to achieve that end. In essence, you're going on a journey together, but each person has a different destination in mind.

The worry is not that some team members are wrong about what they think the team is trying to accomplish. Although it may seem counterintuitive, the worry is that all of the team members may be correct. That is because a crisis cannot be seen comprehensively through a narrow lens. A holistic set of perspectives—a real solution that includes all objectives—is needed.

How might different objectives look when a team wrestles with a product-quality crisis?

* The product manager will concentrate on getting good-quality product to customers as quickly as possible.

* The technical people will focus on how to ensure the product is truly of good quality.

* The public affairs leader will be concerned with the corporate reputation.

* The marketing manager will be worried about the brand reputation.

* The finance manager will be watching the costs.

✱ The attorney will be concerned with future litigation, which in the long run can add costs and damage the corporate and brand reputation.

All are valid. The challenge is to include all of them in order to have the most successful outcome. To define success in terms of just one perspective is to risk compromising others.

⚠ *Pitfall – You're going on a journey together, but each person has a different destination in mind.*

Numerous times I have led a team in a discussion of defining what success would look like. After many such exercises, I realized that the objectives each team created all looked similar despite the fact they were working on different types of crises. Since time is often at a premium, I usually give a team a starter set of objectives and let them modify or add.

✱ **Adhere to or enhance your Core Values–** Good crisis management means first and foremost doing what is right. DuPont always looked to the company's Core Values (Safety and Health, Environmental Stewardship, Respect for People, and Highest Ethics). These Core Values were excellent guides for helping a team sort out the right thing to do, which can be unclear when faced with only difficult options.

✱ **Fix the problem–** For BP, the 2010 crisis in the Gulf of Mexico was never going to be handled until they stopped the oil gushing from the ruptured well on the seafloor. Regardless of what the crisis is, you need to determine the base issue and fix it.

✱ **Protect brand and corporate reputations–** Crises frequently place reputations at risk. A decision that seems expedient in the near-term, might leave a long-lasting scar on your brand.

✱ **Meet customer needs–** A customer's needs are not limited only to getting the product. They also include product quality and maintaining their company's reputation.

✱ **Manage resources wisely**– A company's financial position comes into play in numerous ways during a crisis. Often delivery of products or services is disrupted, thus, disrupting revenue flow. Direct and indirect costs and other resource commitments will be associated with each of the solutions you are considering. In addition, the team needs to think longer term about dynamics such as loss of market share. And in the U.S. in particular, the threat of litigation is frequently a high-dollar concern. All of these financial considerations must be weighed when you compare your options.

After the team has agreed on a set of objectives, write them in a corner of one of the whiteboards in your work room. They will serve you well as guides when you face decision points along the way.

Key Point:

☑ Starter list for common objectives:
- Adhere to or enhance your Core Values
- Fix the problem
- Meet customer needs
- Protect the brand and corporate reputations
- Manage resources wisely

14.3 Decision-making Tool

During many types of crises, the team arrives at one or more points where they must make critical decisions, some big and some relatively small, but critical nonetheless. For some teams, such decisions are made by the dominant personality in the room or perhaps by the senior person. At best, there is some discussion, and when everyone has circled the topic long enough to feel dizzy—but most often when time simply runs out—a decision is made. Sometimes the move is never actually decided upon; it just seems to happen.

Without an organized process for making critical decisions, the team is like a troop of Scouts wandering along a trail in the woods. They come to a fork where paths diverge and somewhat randomly choose a direction. They move on. But moving on is progress only if they are moving in a good direction. In the fog of a crisis, a good direction can be hard to discern.

Key Point:

 Moving on is progress only if the crisis team is moving in a good direction. In the fog of a crisis, a good direction can be hard to discern.

 WAR STORY | **A Dilemma – Chocolate or No Chocolate?**

Imagine the quandary if the decision you are facing involves either stopping sales of all chocolate in the U.S. or leaving the product, some of which contains enough poison to kill a few people, in the marketplace. I got a call one Saturday telling me that was the dilemma. A load of cocoa beans reportedly had been shipped to the U.S. from West Africa in the same overseas shipping container that had carried a hazardous material to the African continent. The concern came to light when the receiver of the cocoa beans complained about white powder on the beans. Examination of the records on that container confirmed that a DuPont product had been in it prior to the beans. While the records were correct, and our product was in fact white, it made no sense that any of our material would have been on the floor of the shipping container, let alone on the beans. Our material was shipped in sturdy vaults, and there had been no reports of any leaks. A technical team quickly was dispatched to the warehouse where we were told the beans in question had been isolated. We wanted to test to see what the white powder was.

When our crew arrived at the warehouse, they were refused entry. They finally managed to talk their way in, only to learn that all of the cocoa beans had been shipped on, with the questionable bags mixed among other bags for processing. Tracking the bags in question was going to be exceedingly difficult, if not impossible.

Nevertheless, we launched a slew of efforts to locate the bags and to gather other information, including what would happen if those beans were processed and used. We teetered on the brink of either calling a halt to chocolate sales altogether or leaving some bags of beans floating around the marketplace unidentified and possibly dangerously contaminated.

Fortunately, before we reached the critical hour, we learned that the white powder in the shipping container was talc. When someone first scanned the records of what had been shipped in that container they missed the form that showed another party had used it to ship talc between our use and the shipping of the cocoa beans. Recall that in Chapter 10 we discussed that during a crisis some information is invariably wrong; this was a classic example. In this case, however, the new information solved the dilemma.

During the chocolate dilemma, I developed some new gray hairs, and I began work on an early version of the Decision-making Matrix, a tool to guide discussion and decision-making using a the multi-faceted set of objectives to define success. Over the years, I continued to refine the tool, and it has proved useful time and again when making tough decisions. The latest version is included here.

Sample Objectives	Option 1	Option 2	Option 3	Option 4
Adhere to/ enhance our core values				
Minimize impacts				
Meet customer needs				
Protect image and brand reputations				
Manage resources wisely				

In the previous section, the importance of setting objectives was discussed. Here we will put those objectives to use. They become guideposts when smoke obscures your vision.

Any decision point implies there is a choice to be made. Invariably there are options for what to do next, but if the group is struggling to decide, that means you are at one of those points where all obvious options have downsides. This sort of critical judgment point is common during a crisis.

Here is a blueprint for how to assess your options and make a decision. But more than that, it is a plan for how to move forward in a good direction or at least choose the best of the bad lot, which often is what is called for.

Asking questions designed to engage the team in creative thinking

First, the group agrees on the objectives of what they are trying to accomplish. Next, the group must agree on what the options are. For example, if one of the choices is to recall the product, what exactly does that mean? All of it? Certain lots? Certain geographies? Or do you really mean a stop sale? Would halting future product sales be sufficient?

One of your choices always should be to "do nothing." While this is seldom a viable option, keeping it in the range is a good benchmark as you weigh the benefits and risks of other options.

After the group has listed the obvious choices, pause to ask about the not-so-obvious choices. Give people permission to be creative. In the sober atmosphere of the work room where it seems you are staring into the abyss, it does not feel natural to get a little crazy with imaginative ideas. But that may be exactly what you need. If all of the alternatives you listed have undesirable characteristics or consequences, take a few minutes to search for something else. When you're lost in the ground-fog, why not climb a tree to see if there is a better view? Invariably, when people are urged to be inventive, they exceed all expectations in what they come up with; they just need to be asked.

Often during a product-quality issue, the default question is posed: Should we recall the product? That question implies it's a yes-or-no decision. Generally both options—recall or don't recall—have dire consequences. The group gets stuck. But as soon as someone asks: "What options do we have other than recalling or not recalling the product?"—the team readily generates options that might exist between yes and no. Often within minutes, they produce five or more new ideas.

Creating the Matrix

Once you have your objectives and a list of obvious and not-so-obvious options, you have the building blocks for making a decision. Now create a matrix with the objectives listed down the left side of a whiteboard and the options written across the top.

Usually a team can fill in the boxes of the matrix in fairly short order. Move across the rows comparing one option to another relative to how each meets that specific objective. Because a room of DuPont people invariably has lots of engineers and scientists, the question quickly arises: Can we rank the options on a scale of 1 to 5? Or a Six Sigma person, who has been trained in data-driven analysis, will ask about using a ranking of 1, 3, and 9. My experience is that if you try to rank the options on some sort of scale, you get tangled up and delayed as the group tries to decide, for example, what a 3 means for the objective of "Meeting customer needs."

Rather than giving each option a score, there is a better approach. I give each of the options a letter: A, B, C . . . G. We fill in the boxes moving across each row of the matrix. First, I ask the group if option A is acceptable and briefly note the answer in the box below the A option, perhaps just "Okay." Then I ask if B is better or worse than A. If, for example, they say B is better than A, I enter B>A in the box under B. Then I ask how C compares to A and B. If C is worse than B, we note in the box for that objective "A<B>C," meaning that for this one objective, A is not as good as (less than) B, and B is better than (greater than) C. At this point in the discussion, option B has the advantage in helping to meet that one objective. We can add a brief mention of the shortcomings or strengths of an option in each box as we discuss its merits relative to that objective. For example, we might cite B as offering the greatest safety.

We move across the rows, discussing each objective and how it would be met or not met by each option. As the matrix is filled in, you usually find that no one option is ideal in meeting all objectives. But you probably already knew that. If there was a perfect choice, the team would have moved forward with that action and would not have been stuck. This tool is used when there is no clear choice.

Although no one option is likely to be perfect, the team may very well find an option or two that have major weaknesses. For example, one option may be highly unfair to the customers. If even one box in a column (option) is significantly bad and the team simply cannot live with that aspect, then that option is eliminated. Rather than erase it from the whiteboard, I put a red X through the box that caused the option to be rejected and draw a red line down through the column. I want us to remember that we considered that option and could not live with that one element. We should not waste any more time talking about that idea. Drawing a line to eliminate an option is valuable in that it reduces the number of viable options.

As you move through the discussions, you likely will see patterns emerge. I create a list of Key Insights on the whiteboard so that we capture them. For example, while leading a team through a decision-making matrix on a critical production and supply-chain problem, I noted how often options were being eliminated because there was not enough time to pursue them. Our customers needed the new product immediately. When I noted on the list of Key Insights that time was a limiting factor in the most viable options, the problem shifted from a production issue to a question of what we might do to allow us more time. Was there a bridging effort that could meet our customer's needs in the short term and buy us the time to implement a better long-term solution? It turned out there was.

The Hybrid Approach

A hybrid approach, where you combine elements of two or more options, sometimes comes to light when you discuss the options. In a situation such as the production/supply-chain example above, someone might say, "What if we employ Option D for about six weeks while we get into position for Option B? We could work with the customers to see whether they can hold on long enough for that to work."

At the end of the process to fill in the matrix, the team usually has narrowed the choices to perhaps a couple that have any hope of adequately meeting the needs. The matrix is then ready for its next use, which is to show it to senior management. One great aspect of the decision-making matrix is that you can bring others into the room, and, at a glance, they can see the range of options you considered and why some have been eliminated. You quickly are ready for a conversation about which of the two or three remaining options you should pursue. Perhaps one requires a significant increase in budget but otherwise is the most positive. Management then must decide whether to provide the added resources called for by that option.

The decision-making matrix has served me well in numerous situations where we were stuck with only truly bad alternatives for dealing with a quandary. The tool is remarkable in its ability to help solve the seemingly unsolvable.

 WAR STORY | **The Opposite of What the Bosses Recommended**

Some years ago, the bosses of our crop protection business told me a significant packaging problem with an insecticide had developed. They instructed me to meet with the team and convince them that the only right thing to do was to recall the product, even though it was going to cost some farmer-customers their crops. Intuitively, our leaders thought about safety and environmental stewardship as the highest priorities.

The product in question was a tried and true insecticide that had been used by farmers for 20 years with excellent results. Then, within a span of two weeks, we received two reports of flames shooting out of the container when a farmer punctured the seal.

The package was like an antifreeze jug with a plastic locking cap and a foil seal that had to be punctured so the liquid could be poured into a spray tank for dilution. Flames shooting from the package seemed impossible, but we had two credible reports, as well as evidence that included a jacket with a burned sleeve. Given our intense commitment to safety, the obvious decision would be to recall the product until we could figure out what was wrong.

Unfortunately, the timing was particularly bad for some farmers in the southwestern U.S. where, if they were not able to apply our insecticide, they would be ruined by an insect invasion that was on the verge of annihilating particular crops. Our field people told us the threat was so serious that the farmers would refuse to hand over the product they had.

When we used the decision-making matrix to analyze our options, it turned out that attempting to recall the product was not going to meet any of our objectives. Clearly, we needed a creative solution. During the discussion, one team member came up with the best idea, built on the theory that the only possible explanation for the flames was a minor change in the foil seal. The theory posited that a static charge built up during shipment. Then, when a farmer punctured the seal with a metal instrument (in the two reports a nail and a pen knife had been used), the spark that was created was enough to ignite the alcohol vapor that sat above the liquid.

I was elected to tell the bosses that their recommendation was a bad idea. Although they were out of town, the bosses quickly understood the reasoning when I described the matrix results over the phone.

Given the okay by senior leaders, the team developed a multi-pronged plan to prevent farmers from getting burned when opening the insecticide they needed to save their crops. We designed a tool—a wooden dowel with a cross beam—for puncturing the seal and hired every wood shop we could find to make thousands of them as quickly as possible. We also had red stop-sign stickers printed to go on every jug: a clear warning not to use a metal tool to break the seal. We over-night shipped the dowels and stickers to all our field people who then went to every agriculture supply store and every farmer they knew, spreading the word as well as opening every carton of jugs to put stickers on the caps and drop in some wooden dowels.

As it turned out, the theory was correct—a slight change in the foil seal had created the possibility of a spark. And thanks to a creative solution engendered by use of the decision-making tool, no one was burned, and the crops were saved.

14.4 Pause & Reflect Tool

Sometimes I was parachuted into a room where a team had been laboring for days or weeks and finally determined they needed assistance to find their way out of the tangled briars. The Pause & Reflect tool can be an effective means for helping to resolve a thorny problem that has been resistant to all efforts to date.

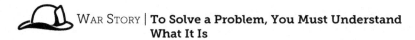 WAR STORY | **To Solve a Problem, You Must Understand What It Is**

A business leader set up a team to deal with a sophisticated product-counterfeiting problem. When the crisis management team seemed to be getting nowhere in addressing the problem, he asked me for assistance.

I was not made to feel welcome when I arrived, though. "We know the boss sent you to help us, so tell us your solution," the team leader demanded.

I suggested we use the Pause & Reflect tool to help clarify the problem being addressed.

The reply was frosty: "No, thanks. We already know what problem we're dealing with. We need you to tell us how to solve it." At the end of some pushing and pulling, I told them that if, in fact, they had a good grip on the situation, it would not take much time for my approach. They grudgingly began the exercise, but the more they talked, the more they argued among themselves. It ultimately took them two full weeks to agree on what the problem was. No wonder they were struggling to find a solution.

The Pause & Reflect tool allows an outside resource like me to come up to speed quickly without unduly wasting the team's time. Also, when conditions change substantially, as they sometimes do, the P&R tool allows everyone to step back to reassess exactly what problem the team is trying to address. The results of the process can be kept on the whiteboard and periodically revisited.

Step 1 — Getting the Holistic View

At the outset, the Pause & Reflect tool takes a quick look at the situation from the perspectives of key stakeholders such as customers, competitors, regulators, elected officials, industry associations, local community, senior management and employees, as well as traditional and social media. The point of asking for various points of view at the beginning of the process is to enable the team to see the whole picture objectively in order to understand the scope of the problem and to find a solution for the entire situation, not just a few parts of it.

Key Point:

☑ Typical list of key stakeholders for P&R tool:
- Customers
- Competitors
- Regulators
- Elected Officials
- Industry Associations
- Local Community
- Senior Management
- Employees
- Traditional and Social Media

Using the "Pause" function: Assessing where we are now

The "Pause" function, much like the pause button on a video

player, yields a freeze-frame that captures the situation at one particular moment. That step alone is helpful because it gives all of the people on the Core Team a chance to describe how the situation is viewed in their arenas. For example, the person who is interacting with regulatory agencies takes a few minutes to update the team on how the regulators currently see the problem. Unless there is a topic that requires a more in-depth group discussion, five minutes or so per stakeholder group should be sufficient.

Begin by listing the stakeholders on a whiteboard. Ask team members to describe the perspectives of their groups. Write each of the key details on the board as a bullet point. At the end of the round of comments, add the date. If you have available room on the whiteboards, leave the stakeholder views up for a while; they serve as useful benchmarks for gauging how things change. Because a crisis can move in increments, it is easy to lose track of how much it can shift, even over a period as short as just a week or two.

Step 2 — Using the "Reflect" function: Projecting the future

Once you have finished the initial holistic review of the situation, the next step is scenario planning. Begin by asking the team how the crisis might develop: Best Case, Probable Case, and Worst Case. First, you will need to agree on the time interval of the projection. For some situations, the farthest out you will be able to project might be a week or two, especially if there are critical events that will occur in that period. In other situations, you will want to look out further, sometimes as much as a few years.

This step is a rapid version of a scenario planning process, one that can be done in less than two hours. Certainly there are many techniques for scenario planning, including some that are much more detailed and elaborate. The benefits of the Pause & Reflect approach are that it can be done quickly and that it will move you immediately to strategic action. In the midst of a crisis there is seldom time for extensive scenario planning.

The scenario planning step begins by asking: Given where we are today, what is the Worst Case scenario that could develop in the coming week (two weeks, a month...whatever timeframe you have chosen)? Especially in the American culture, people often need to talk about the terrible things that could happen before they feel free to be more optimistic. So first ask, if everything went really badly, what would that look like? Create a bulleted list of key factors in a column on the right side of your whiteboard. It must be a holistic list, so it will include, for example, what the news media will be reporting, what your customers will be doing, how your competitors will react, the class-action lawsuits that will be filed, and the fines levied by regulators.

Next ask the group: If everything goes really well, what might that look like? Again, for this Best Case scenario, you want a holistic view. Put the bulleted list for this projection in a column on the left side of your whiteboard. The team will want to know if they can include positive outcomes that they could help make happen. The answer is "yes." In fact, that will be the first step after you have articulated all three scenarios. You will be looking for opportunities where the team can positively influence the future.

After you have listed specific outcomes of the Worst Case and Best Case, create a Probable Case column between the two. I have never had a situation where the Probable Case scenario looked like the Best Case projection—it most likely would not have been a crisis in that instance. I have, however, experienced a crisis in which the Probable Case scenario looked essentially identical to the Worst Case projection. Figuratively speaking, everything was on fire around us, and every key stakeholder with any power was against us.

Step 3 – Influencing the future

The next step in Pause & Reflect is to ask what the team can do to influence the future. Again, you want to begin with the Worst Case scenario. Look at the bullet points in that column. Which are the most crucial? And where might the team have some ability to influence that potential impact? Circle those items and talk about how to "play defense." How can team actions keep the future from emerging in such a negative fashion? List strategic actions that could influence the future.

Next, move to the Best Case scenario. Circle the items that are most crucial and where the team might be able to drive to a positive outcome. List how to "play offense" in strategic team actions.

"We saved the company $10,000 by not asking for more resources. Unfortunately, it ended up costing us almost a million as a result."
—Stu Poore, Crisis Production Leader, Gudenuff Technology

A "lean and mean" mentality is the normal mode of operation at many companies. I remind teams in a crisis situation that this is not a normal time. It might be foolish, for example, to fail to ask for needed resources, however costly, that might help avoid a huge negative for the corporation. Ask the participants to consider what help they may need.

Key Point:

☑ Managing a crisis is not business as usual. It might be foolish to fail to mobilize resources that would allow you to avoid a huge negative for the company.

As you examine the list of Strategic Actions and make assignments, be sure you are bringing all needed resources to bear. Do not be constrained by assuming that you are limited to what you see in the room. When you show the scenarios to management, make the case for the needed resources. Enlist their help as you seek to take control of the situation.

Step 4 – Expectation management

The Pause & Reflect tool helps the team frame where the crisis is likely headed, and it is also useful when reviewing the situation with senior leaders. The importance of expectation management begins with senior leaders. They deserve to know what could be coming. The three columns on your whiteboard give them a look at your current thinking in that regard.

The Best Case column shows management that the problem is not likely to go away, and certainly not without concerted effort. Similarly, the Worst Case column helps management understand that the situation could get quite bad, especially if nothing is done to try to steer it in a different direction. The Probable Case lets the leaders see what the future likely holds. Reviewing the three columns leads to discussion of your recommended Strategic Actions and your requests for any added resources.

14.5 Stakeholder Assessment Quadrants

A simple four-quadrant chart can help your team visualize the position of each of the key stakeholders. Draw a vertical line and label the top end "For" and the bottom end "Against." Across the middle of your vertical line draw a horizontal line. On the right end write "Active" and on the left end write "Inactive."

Look at your list of key stakeholders and ask the team to place each one somewhere on the chart. The discussion about where each stakeholder group goes is a healthy assessment of where the key parties stand on the topic. You may find that an entity you were considering as a unified group is not altogether homogenous and that you need to split it into sub-groups. For example, different customers may view the situation differently. Likewise federal regulators may end up in different places. Even individuals within a stakeholder group may be in different places. This is a rich conversation that yields significant insights regarding who and what you are really facing in your crisis.

In virtually every crisis, you will have stakeholders who are actively against you. Place them in the lower right quadrant. Intuitively, team members will wonder how to get those stakeholders to be actively for you.

The sad news is that people usually don't move like that *(Figure 1)*. They must travel the long way around, becoming first inactively against you, then inactively for you *(Figure 2)*. Only in rare instances will anyone make the whole journey from actively against you to actively for you. If they do, they become a powerful ally *(Figure 3)*. But again, that is highly unlikely. Moreover, the

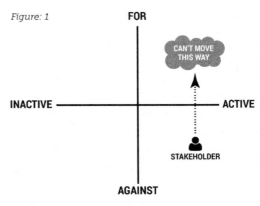

Figure: 1

effort required to promote such a dramatic shift may steal valuable time and energy from your team that would be better directed elsewhere.

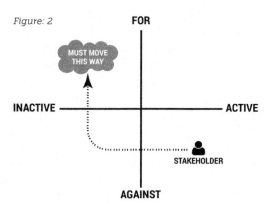

Figure: 2

The good news is that it may be sufficient for stakeholders to move to the lower left quadrant where they still do not like you and what has happened, but they become less vocal in the public discourse *(Figure 4)*. If you show good faith efforts to fix the problem and work to rebuild trust, they may take a lower profile as they watch events unfold.

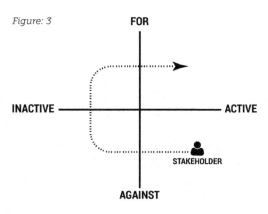

Figure: 3

The four quadrants provide a visual rendition of how the key stakeholders sort out. You readily can see those you might count as allies and those who are your most strident detractors. This array will help the team understand the work that is before them as they strive to make progress on solving the problem and communicating about it.

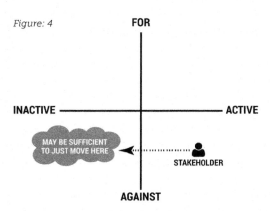

Figure: 4

CHAPTER

15

Managing a Crisis in Social Media

What's In This Chapter:

15.1 Three Phases: Monitoring, Analyzing, Engaging

Social media, such as Facebook, Twitter, YouTube, and the many other channels, have caused a major shift in the way individuals communicate with each other and in the way companies interact with individuals. Gone are the days when communication was largely from the top down and word went out mainly through a news release. Instead, communication is multi-layered, interactions are multi-directional, and transmission of information, news and opinion is instantaneous. Social media have become the go-to channel for many of your stakeholders to convey or exchange information and to comment on a crisis as it is happening.

If you are not already well versed in communicating through social media, a crisis is a bad time to start, and you may want to hire some outside help. A word of caution, though: Make sure you confirm that the individual or organization you are hiring has done work through social media relative to crisis communications. Many people may tell you they can handle it, but you need to check references and ask probing questions before hiring someone to help in this strategic role.

The task of assessing and responding to social media in relation to a crisis is a complicated mission. It is helpful to think of it in three phases:

* Monitoring
* Analyzing
* Engaging

Each phase has distinct challenges and requisite skills and knowledge.

Monitoring

Attempting to monitor social media during an active crisis quickly can bury you in data that are almost impossible to sort in meaningful ways. You easily can end up being data rich but insight poor. There are numerous social media filtering, tracking, and monitoring tools to help you. Prices for social media monitoring tools range from free to costly. Begin by reading current online reviews and talking to vendors. The landscape continues to change rapidly in available tools and techniques, so stick with the most recent assessments you can find.

Using the tools requires dedicated time and special knowledge, particularly because of the volume of material. Begin by designating "keywords" that will extract those posts most relevant to your issue. In a high-profile crisis, you will accumulate a blizzard of information. The next question is: What does it mean?

Analyzing

Depending on the monitoring program you set up, you should have a jump on analysis. The core question is: "What is the impact?"

There are various technologies and techniques for judging what matters and what essentially is background noise. If you determine that a trend in social media probably does matter, the next question is: "What should we do about it?"

Engaging

Corporations, traditionally hierarchical, structured, and closed, find themselves, thanks to the big bang of social media, in a new universe—one that is interactive and open. Companies still clinging to a world where you send out a press release to some select news media when you want to communicate are in for a rude awakening when it comes to engaging through social media. It is not that you can throw out the old approach—it still matters— but you will have to incorporate new dimensions regarding how you interact with stakeholders.

The good news is that if done well, you can increase your effectiveness in communicating. You can become much more targeted in reaching those who really care. Plus, you take out the middle filters of the reporters who are writing the stories and the editors who are changing them. You get to go directly to the stakeholders with your message.

Social media have their own protocols, and you need to fit your style to those norms. For example, once you decide to engage, you need to remain engaged. Make a commitment to see the issue through and be part of the conversation. Flinging one comment into the mix and then fleeing often will do more harm than good. Also, you need to stay with the discussion in real time. Checking for comments only every few days will likely miss the mark. Indeed, it may suggest to some that you do not really care about communicating with them.

 "I learned the hard way that you shouldn't take a blog to a Twitter fight."
—Stu Poore, Crisis Production Leader, Gudenuff Technology

In addition, you need to know that you must address the situation on the channel where the action is taking place. If the interactions are on YouTube, it doesn't help much to start a blog. If the exchanges are occurring on Twitter, that's where you need to be with your messages as part of the conversation.

Traditional Media versus Social Media:

Traditional Media	Social Media
Controlled release	Interactive
Formal	Informal
Deliberate	Rapid fire
One and done	Ongoing engagement

People joke that senior leaders need to hire a twenty-something to teach them how to work with social media. To a degree that is true. Younger employees have grown up within the online community and are much more comfortable with it at the tactical level. The challenge is how to merge those tactics with the strategic needs of managing a crisis.

Essentially, every crisis has a social media element. To imagine that you will be able to ignore those dynamics is naïve and dangerous. Ideally, you and the team will become familiar with social media in the calm before the storm and then will have a comfort level as well as some skills when the storm arrives.

Preparation is key when communicating important information

When a crisis erupts, no matter where, no matter when, stakeholders will be waiting for answers. Just as with traditional media, it is important to be prepared to communicate successfully through social media.

❋ Be ready. When a problem arises, be prepared to implement a planned strategy such as using Twitter to get the basics of the situation into the news and directly to stakeholders.

❋ Follow up. After the initial message, communicate often with regular and consistent messages. Also, watch for ad hoc groups to pop up on social media and be ready to engage with them.

❋ Be accurate, credible, and inclusive as well as timely. Bring in subject-matter experts if need be to help explain the nature of the crisis. Helping employees, government officials, or the public understand the situation assists in allaying fears, reducing stress, and building relationships. Address any rumors. Involve stakeholders.

✱ Be consistent. As stated previously, tying your statements to your Core Values will maintain continuity throughout the crisis and will help stakeholders know that you are guided by your principles.

Key Point:

☑ Written comments in social media lack the tone of voice of a spoken comment. Humor and irony can be dangerous because they easily—and even purposefully—can be misinterpreted.

15.2 The Whipsaw Effect: Traditional Media and Social Media

There is a whipsaw effect when a crisis is headlined in traditional media as well as social media, which is frequently the case. Like the lumbermen's saw, the topic moves back and forth rapidly between the two.

People imagine that social media catalyze the ping-pong effect. While that can happen, more often it is newspaper, radio, and television coverage that launches the social media buzz. In fact, if you look at time charts of social media activity on a hot topic, they often show spikes immediately following the evening news.

In turn, social media can drive further coverage in traditional media. People commenting on Twitter may post new information or new angles that are picked up and reported on in print or in the electronic press. Reporters monitor social media closely when a crisis is breaking or evolving.

15.3 Digital Witnesses are Everywhere

People all over the world have smart phones, ready to record anything that happens. On any subway or sidewalk, in every car, hospital or shop, there is a person with a smartphone who has the capability to record any event. Instantly, those images and words— photos, videos, sound recordings—can be uploaded to YouTube,

Facebook, or any other social networking site, essentially making them available to the whole world.

In addition to handheld units, there are security cameras in every parking lot and store and on many street corners. Our lives are being recorded all the time.

The famous photo of the US Airways Flight 1549 that was landed masterfully in the Hudson River by Captain C. B. "Sully" Sullenberger, shows people standing on the wings of the plane awaiting rescue. First, we should recognize that there were lots of photos taken of the "miracle on the Hudson" scene, which is not unusual but merits recognition of the ubiquitous nature of recording devices. Second, the people standing on the wings of the airplane in the frigid river are themselves texting and tweeting, witnessing even as they wonder if they will survive. The photo is a stark reminder of the dynamics of digital media in a crisis situation.

US Airways Flight 1549 in the Hudson River, New York, USA on 15 January 2009
PHOTO BY GREG L -ORIGINALLY POSTED TO FLICKR AS PLANE CRASH INTO HUDSON RIVER

Your employees, customers, and adversaries all have the capability of recording and publishing what they witness. Animal rights activists, for example, have managed to get inside livestock facilities and animal testing labs in order to record what people generally know is happening but would prefer not to see. And, of course, that is the exact point of the activists—to show people what is happening and hope at least some will object.

Key Point:

☑ Images of a crisis are powerful and permanent. Expect them.

Almost any crisis has the potential for someone to record and publish images or descriptions of what they witnessed. Furthermore, you have to be ready for rapid dissemination. Other stakeholders, perhaps harboring unrelated concerns, might use the content for their own objectives. For example a labor union might try to capitalize on an environmental incident to drive home what is largely a separate point.

Images of a crisis are powerful and permanent. Expect them. You will not be able to prevent them, but you can be ready to deal with them.

15.4 Challenges of Language and Culture

Discussions through social media occur, of course, in the language of the participants. An issue in Brazil is discussed in Portuguese, while a controversy in Italy is debated in Italian. Some topics that cross national or international borders find a common language. Often that language is English, but not necessarily. A crisis that generates broad interest may be discussed simultaneously in many languages. Monitoring, analyzing and engaging in multiple languages—and doing it in real time on an ongoing basis—is a major challenge. Consider, though, that some of the time-saving software monitoring and filtering tools mentioned above can monitor not only across several social media platforms but also across multiple languages.

For some companies, especially those with direct, online interactions with consumers throughout the world, there already may be an infrastructure that can be tapped during a crisis. For many companies, though, there is not a ready-made arrangement. You may have some building blocks though. Multinational firms have employees in many countries, and those native speakers of the local language can be asked to help monitor what is being said in the social media. They may even be able to provide some rudimentary analysis. Asking them to engage may be another story, however. Turning employees loose to have a dialogue through social media about a controversial topic may lead to more problems than it solves.

One piece of analysis you will need relates to the cultural context of the online conversation. The discussion among native-born citizens of a country in their own language occurs in the context of their culture and social norms. Dynamics, such as what is appropriate in the way of humor, sarcasm, and criticism of public officials, are so ingrained that we may not consciously think of them at all when we have discourse. Yet those dynamics are an essential part of the meaning of a comment in the culture. Without someone to sift through statements and provide the real meaning, an outsider's interpretation of comments can be faulty and even dangerous.

Because a crisis can flare so quickly, building the capacity to monitor, analyze, and engage in key countries around the world must be done in advance. In a real-world crisis, it would be almost impossible to create this surge capacity quickly and effectively.

Contractors such as communications firms may have a network in place that you can tap into for use during your crisis. Assessing your needs and the available services in advance is a wise move if your vulnerability assessment indicates you may require such assistance.

15.5 Decision Trees

The step between Analyzing and Engaging is big and difficult to navigate. It is complicated to know how much and what type of traffic matters. It is even more complex to know how much effect the online conversation is having and whether that conversation warrants your engagement.

Various decision trees are publicly available online and may assist you in your thinking about when, where, and how to engage. Your decision tree probably does not need to be immensely complicated or technical, but you do need one. Having an assessment process thought out in advance will allow you to gauge the situation in the heat of a crisis and, at a minimum, be able to rule some choices in or out, thus simplifying your decision making on whether to engage.

15.6 Measuring Your impact

It is even more complex to know how much influence the online conversation is having and whether that conversation warrants your engagement. There are scoring systems that help calibrate the impact of streams of comments based on the influence of the people who are doing the commenting. Klout Score is an example of a system used to determine how much sway an individual has.

There are also tools for plotting trends so that you can see whether you are having any impact through social media. The tools you employ for analysis may provide you with insights on whether your engagement is having a positive effect. Use of social media is highly dynamic and merits ongoing analysis for the duration of the crisis.

CHAPTER

16

Aftermath

What's In This Chapter:

16.1 What Does a Win Look Like?

When a crisis starts to fade in the rearview mirror, many teams conclude that the crisis was a pass-fail test. I have seen teams celebrate "victory" after what, by any measure, was a terrible response to a crisis. After encountering this disconnect a few times, I started to wonder why those celebrations were happening. My primary conclusion is that because they survived, the team members considered their effort at crisis management a success. The business was still there, and they still had their jobs; therefore, they must have done well.

Research shows that most crises do not completely destroy a company. Crises can severely damage companies, but they seldom cause them to go out of business. Likewise, careers can be damaged, but unless people have done something illegal or in violation of the company's Core Values, they likely will not lose their jobs.

To be clear, crisis management is not pass-fail. Grades occur along what would look like a classic bell curve. Few companies would get an A+. People talk about Johnson & Johnson's recall of Extra Strength Tylenol® as the model. Actually, J&J was the victim, not the culprit; someone else put cyanide in the pain-relief capsules. Regardless, the decision to conduct a broad recall was a ground-breaking move, but the inside story, as I understand it, is that it was a move that was slow in coming and somewhat backed into. Certainly, if J&J learned anything from the experience, it is not obvious, because they have stumbled time and again with other product-quality problems that appear to be largely of their own making.

The irony about getting an A+ in managing a crisis is that when you do a first-class job, people on the outside—including people within the company but outside your crisis team—may never know there was a problem. Of course, that usually is one of the hoped-for outcomes. There is no doubt that some crisis-response efforts can be considered "A work," but in the midst of all the struggles and tough decisions, it may be difficult to discern, especially from the outside.

There is also "F work," to be sure. Some have argued that Penn State University deserves an F for its handling of the sexual-abuse allegations related to an assistant football coach. Others have judged that British Petroleum did very poorly when managing the oil spill in the Gulf of Mexico.

The performance of most companies in dealing with a major crisis, though, falls somewhere along the middle of the bell curve. There can be no precise grading without being inside a crisis room, knowing what choices had to be made and what possibly could have happened but didn't. Simply observing actions from the outside does not tell you what any of the other crisis response choices were.

My advice: when a crisis winds down, do not give your team a grade—give them an education. Chapter 17 describes how to capture lessons from the experience. Make sure the team learns and improves, and then share the lessons, as appropriate, throughout the company.

Key Point:

....

☑ When a crisis winds down, do not give your team a grade—give them an education.

....

16.2 People Want to Do Business with a Company that Knows How to Manage a Crisis

The paradox of having survived a crisis—particularly if it was successfully managed—can be that other companies may see your enterprise as a more desirable firm with which to do business. Smart business leaders realize that preparation is key, because it is not a matter of if their company will have a crisis, but rather when they will have one. Thus, they want to do business with companies that know how to handle themselves in crisis mode.

Imagine that, having recently done a product recall, you write up the case study and share your hard-won insights. By offering your expertise to your customer base, you raise their level of understanding and enhance your reputation in the process. Clearly, your company is better off for the experience and may even capitalize on it.

CASE STUDY | **When it Absolutely, Positively Has to Get There Overnight—or Over the Fence**

FedEx experienced a worst-case crisis in 2011 when a video, recorded by a home security camera, went viral with millions of views on YouTube. The twenty-second clip shows a FedEx driver "delivering" a computer monitor by launching it over a fence. To make matters worse, the Grinch-like incident happened right in the middle of the December holidays. FedEx boldly shared the case study with other companies so that all could learn. In the process, they solidified the image of FedEx as a company that knows how to step up to a crisis.

....

During the years I worked at DuPont, there was an ongoing parade of customers who visited our headquarters to learn how the company handled crisis management. DuPont added value to the customers' businesses by sharing its expertise. That, in turn, added value to DuPont, because its customers would be better prepared when a crisis struck them.

16.3 Rewarding Behavior—Risks and Rewards of Giving Awards for Crisis Response

When the crisis is over there can be a desire to recognize those who fought the fire. Those people put in long hours and shouldered the burdens of the struggle. But despite good intentions, significant harm can occur if recognition is not given in a coordinated and thoughtful manner. I have seen some sad situations where acknowledgment was so mismanaged that people were demoralized and hurt. I actually have heard people say that because of the way recognition was handled they never would participate in a crisis response again.

....

"In the madness of the day, recognition of the positive is sometimes compromised."
—Paul Dice, Crisis Management Expert

....

General Guidance for giving recognition and awards

✱ Timing matters when acknowledging the efforts of individuals. Doing something quickly is preferable to taking many months to get it perfect, so don't over-complicate the process and thus slow it down. Research shows that a sincere and prompt hand-written "Thank You!" carries as much impact as a fancy dinner a few months later or a trip to Disney World a year after the fact.

✱ Until you know how you will handle all of the commendations that might be warranted, however, avoid the temptation to do a one-off formal recognition, such as holding a thank-you lunch or presenting any sort of a tangible memento like a certificate. I have seen situations where some leaders have held a "special dinner" or provided a "special compensation award" for a select group. When word gets out (as it always does), questions arise and feelings of those who may have been left out are hurt.

✱ Something tangible is important. Note how often people have recognition items still hanging on their office walls or sitting on their desks. People treasure the fact that someone appreciated their efforts. I have seen crisis team members change offices and in the new office pin up, yet again, a yellowed note that simply expresses thanks.

✱ A verbal "thank you" is always appropriate. When thanking individuals in any sort of a public forum (even a conference call), it is a good idea to broaden the point to say, "and there were many others who also contributed to this successful response."

✱ Be aware that people who were not part of the team often picked up part of the regular work of those who were on the team. Those who took up the slack should be considered for recognition as well.

✱ When in doubt about whether to include someone in the acknowledgments, be inclusive.

Here are three recognition options (in order of increasing complexity) that can work:

Option 1— Arrange blanket recognition so that all contributors are treated equally. This kind of attention can be in the form of a certificate or a small memento. For our 2009 pandemic response effort, we gave an inexpensive Lucite globe with a thank-you letter.

Option 2— Carry out #1, but add some special lunches. Again, when in doubt about whether to include someone, be inclusive.

Option 3— To acknowledge the extra effort of those who shouldered the most responsibility, put in the longest hours, and accomplished the more difficult work, create three levels of recognition. This approach assures that you are not inadvertently disregarding the other contributors while you recognize those who carried the heaviest loads:

Levels of Recognition Chart

Level	Contributor	Extra Effort	Heavy Lifting
Description	People who helped with the effort in any manner.	People who put in added effort, such as off-hours work, not just once or twice but on an ongoing basis.	These are the people who carried a lot of the responsibility day after day.
Examples	People who jumped in for a short period when asked. People who backed up those who were pulled onto the formal team.	People who gave up personal time on a frequent basis and who made substantial contributions to the effort.	Members of the central team who contributed day-in and day-out. They shouldered the stress and burden.
Type of Recognition	Certificates or small mementos, plus possibly a group lunch.	Certificates or small mementos, plus a financial award. At a minimum, the financial award should be a "Night on the Town" so they can spend time with their families.	Certificates or small mementos, plus significant financial awards.
Remarks	If you are not sure whether to include someone, be inclusive. If you are not sure whether they belong in this category or the next one because it's a borderline case, put them in the next one.	If you are not sure whether they belong in this category or the next one, put them in the next one.	

CHAPTER

17

Learning

What's In This Chapter:

17.1 Debrief Processes

The work your team does in responding to a crisis is an expensive experience. And because no two situations are the same, you purchase an education each time they respond. You will get the benefit of that education only if you establish a process to aid the effort to capture and share the lessons learned. Various organizations use different terms for that process: debrief, post mortem, or after-action report. They mean largely the same thing. I use debrief here for the sake of simplicity.

Key Point:

☑ When entering the debrief process, tread cautiously. Evaluating the positives requires sensitivity lest certain people be given an undue portion of the credit while the contributions of others go unnoticed.

In all probability, the team did some things well. The debrief process allows you to capture those positive points, but it also identifies where the team could have done better. It is important to note the positive outcomes as well as the areas for improvement.

Curiously, the positives may not be as easy to see as the negatives. The positives often are taken for granted to such a degree that they fade into the background. For example, perhaps someone on the Core Team encountered a serious family emergency just when the crisis was hitting a peak of activity, and the team rallied to cover for that person so he or she could attend to the family problem. The reaction might be, "Well, of course, we had to do that." Regardless of whether you felt you had to, you did. That's what good teams do. It not only showed caring and support for the team member with the family problem, but it also sent a message to others that the team would be there for them too.

Key Point:

☑ The negatives are often much easier to spot than the things that were done well.

The negatives are much easier to spot. They have an ugly glower and a lingering stench. The difficulty with some negatives is that they get associated with one or a few people. Sometimes it is glaringly obvious who is to blame for a major misstep. Use caution, though, because some things that appear to be patently clear are not necessarily what they seem. Some people are clever at shifting blame. Or perhaps there is an unknown backstory. Be careful that you do not hurt yourself and others by jumping to conclusions. Take the time to understand fully before taking any action.

 "No wonder the project was a disaster. Just look at who worked on it."
—Stu Poore, Crisis Production Leader, Gudenuff Technology

Whenever I conducted a debrief, I said at the start of the process: "A productive debrief cannot be seen as a finger-pointing exercise." I structured each meeting to make sure we did not inadvertently point to individuals.

In relation to the negatives, the blame may lie beneath the obvious. If someone did something unethical—not in error or out of fatigue but clearly knew what they were doing was wrong—the team would expect that serious misstep to be dealt with by management. For example, if someone had crucial information but did not divulge it because they feared personal embarrassment and having withheld the information set up the team for larger problems, then that error in judgment must be handled by upper management.

In the debriefs, keep in mind that how the negatives are handled will send strong signals to the team and even to people who were not working on the crisis. If others get the message that the crisis team had been set up to fail and then was punished for it, the next time you have a crisis, few will want to be part of the response effort.

"That's the sort of thing that leaves a memory stain. It will never go away."
—Rick Deadwyler, Crisis Management Expert

If at all possible, it is helpful to have a neutral person facilitate the debrief discussion. In the interest of promoting candor, the facilitator should not be a senior leader. In fact, it may be helpful not to have a big boss in the room at all.

"The path to a strong performance may be a near-death experience."
—Linda Fisher, Corporate Executive

The following steps will lead the team through an objective assessment of how they performed. The questions listed highlight specific areas I have seen that are key to success or failure. Note that not all questions are pertinent to every situation.

Guide for a Successful Debrief

Ground rules:

* A debrief is NOT "finger pointing" but rather an opportunity to learn and improve.

* All participants must adhere to legal and ethical guidelines.

Crisis management process assessment:

* Was a team clearly designated?

* Was a team leader clearly designated?

* Was a process leader (facilitator), who was not already serving another function on the team, designated?

* Was the decision-making process clear and efficient?

* Were objectives clearly defined?

* Were decisions reached and implemented in a timely manner?

* Did the team make a conscious effort to look forward in time to anticipate possible developments?

* Were appropriate resources brought to bear in a timely fashion?

* Were roles clearly defined?

* Was there minimal, inappropriate duplication of roles?

* Was an appropriate schedule of meetings lined out?

Information management assessment:

* Was the topic of records management clearly addressed early in the process?

* Was the need for rumor control addressed?

* Was a system established for monitoring and reporting on developments?

* Was management kept appropriately informed and involved?

* Were other people kept appropriately informed?

Process learnings:

Was a process in place to prevent/address this sort of situation?

If Yes:

* Was the process followed?

* Did it work?

- Did we operate at an optimal level?
- Were the right people involved?
- Did we respond in a timely manner?

If No:

✳ Is a process needed?

✳ What elements should it entail?

✳ Absent a formal process, was our response appropriate?

Debrief Summary

What should we:

✳ Keep Doing?

✳ Modify?

✳ Stop Doing?

✳ Start Doing?

Action items:

✳ What?

✳ Who?

✳ When?

Some situations merit more involved debriefs. After the one-two punch of hurricanes Katrina and Rita, we conducted 16 debriefs on various aspects of our response.

More elaborate processes are available to conduct an "after-action assessment." Bear in mind, however, that the same folks who have just been overworked for an extended period of time are the same ones you are asking to spend additional time on the debrief. Be sure that your process aligns with the need.

....

> *"You may not realize it when it happens, but a kick in the teeth may be the best thing in the world for you."*
> —*Walt Disney*

....

17.2 Electronic Surveys

During the 2009 H1N1 pandemic, we had scores of teams mobilized around the world. We wanted to provide each of them a chance to debrief, plus we wanted to be able to aggregate the results so they could be used to improve our larger process and also be shared with the senior leaders of the corporation. In order to manage such a large-scale evaluation, we employed an electronic survey tool to supplement the discussions. We also used this technique to debrief after the somewhat less complicated crisis response to the 2011 Japanese earthquake, tsunami, and nuclear power plant disaster.

Various electronic-survey tools are available. Some that are perfectly useful are free. You also can pay to enhance them with additional capabilities. SurveyMonkey is an example of an electronic-survey instrument.

For an involved response like the H1N1 pandemic, we created a set of survey questions and grouped them into categories: mobilizing, communicating, resource deployment, and compliance with the Core Values. Teams all over the world used the standard set of questions as a discussion guide, and then sent us a completed survey that represented their analysis. Using the electronic tool, we tabulated the responses from the teams and created bar charts of the results. We put the charts in a PowerPoint presentation that was used to enhance a discussion of areas of strengths and weaknesses with senior management.

Using an electronic survey helps the various teams by giving them a structure for the debrief discussion as well as an easy way to send in their results. Plus it helps the central team compile the information. With minimal time and cost, you can capture the lessons of the response and work them into improvements for ongoing crisis preparedness.

17.3 Recounting Lessons Learned

Presenting the lessons from select crisis response efforts can prevent the broader organization from relearning the same costly lessons over and over. There are, however, sensitivities to consider.

First, be careful not to inadvertently make people look bad. By airing the opportunities for improvement, you are publicizing areas where the team did not do as well as it might have. Those communications are valuable but must be done with the caveat that in some instances there were factors that prevented the team from performing optimally.

....

> *"It's clear that we were naïve, persistent and arrogant. That's a deadly combination."*
>
> —*Silvio DeCarli, Senior Attorney*

....

A second sensitivity in reporting the lessons learned is that any litigation associated with a crisis often extends well beyond the time the team disbands. Because debrief documents created by you or others could be subject to the discovery process and could impact the legal proceedings, discuss the legal implications with your attorney before conducting the debrief and developing any written materials.

17.4 Connection to Stewardship

At the beginning of this book, we discussed the importance of good stewardship in preventing crises. When you conduct your debrief after an actual crisis response, you very well may highlight areas where the entire crisis, or at least a portion of it, might have been prevented through enhanced stewardship. Perhaps a more robust

Stewardship is the best investment

The goal is always crisis prevention.

quality-control process would have caught a product defect before the goods ever made it to the marketplace. Or maybe product tracking mechanisms would have allowed you to better target the recall.

"Sometimes you have to mess up to wake up."
—Archie Manning

Look hard at the lessons of the whole experience and loop back to your stewardship programs while the experience is fresh in the minds of everyone, especially the senior leaders. Before the details of the experience fade, show what the crisis cost and compare that figure to what a stewardship program to prevent it would have cost. When you tally up all the numbers, including lost sales, staff time, lawyer fees, claims settlements, and reputation damage, the price of prevention usually looks like a bargain.

CHAPTER

18

Conclusions

What's In This Chapter:

18.1 Prevention is the Best Investment
18.2 Collaboration
18.3 Listen for Early Warning Signals
18.4 Don't Over-reach on Rhetoric
18.5 Crisis Prevention and Preparedness

18.1 Prevention is the Best Investment

In retrospect, it is usually clear that to have prevented a major crisis would have been far better than to have had to deal with the costs, headaches, and damage to reputation that occurred. The challenge is how to achieve that clarity of thought in advance of the catastrophe. For the Deepwater Horizon oil rig explosion and subsequent 87-day gusher in the Gulf of Mexico, the value of prevention was recognized much too late. In terms of dollars and reputation, the disaster cost BP, Halliburton, and Transocean dearly: 11 people were killed, and the oil spill had a massive and lasting effect on the environment and communities all along the Gulf Coast. After the fact, overreaching in timing and technology clearly was a short-sighted approach.

There is never enough money to do everything that might be done in the way of stewardship, but some efforts stand out as high priorities. When conducting your Stewardship Assessments and Vulnerability Assessments, do them with eyes wide open to those priorities. Also, pay close attention to what your crisis exercises teach you. Capitalize on the opportunities to prevent problems.

18.2 Collaboration

You must build relationships before you need them. Like banking, you must make deposits before you can make withdrawals. Whether they are regulators, neighbors, customers, or employees, get to know these stakeholder groups before a crisis erupts. Invest time to meet with key parties. Explain what your business does, and make sure to take time to listen to their views. Work hard to understand their perspectives. Then, when a crisis occurs, you will know and perhaps even trust each other. Such relationship building cannot be done after a crisis begins.

18.3 Listen for Early Warning Signals

When a crisis is analyzed in retrospect, many times it becomes obvious that, in fact, warning signals that foreshadowed a potential crisis were ignored. Make it a priority to listen to the rumblings and set up systems to deal with small problems before they become big ones.

18.4 Don't Overreach on Rhetoric

While some companies seem to do a great deal of self-promoting, the DuPont corporate culture was more inclined toward less of that. Some people say that tendency harkened back to the du Pont family and their approach. As individuals and as a family, they were inclined to do good things but were not disposed to talk about those efforts.

Any hyperbole in rhetoric can come back to haunt you during a crisis. A great example was the BP campaign to change the meaning and perception of BP from British Petroleum to Beyond Petroleum after some exceptionally high-visibility disasters. Many said that BP would have been better served by working to manage petroleum well before moving beyond it.

18.5 Crisis Prevention and Preparedness

Smokejumpers and all firefighters work on prevention as well as on preparedness. They strive to educate people on the value of prevention, but they know that blazes can erupt without warning, leaving no time to get ready. They equip, they train, and they practice, so that when the call comes in they are ready to go.

Despite all of your company's best efforts to prevent problems, crises will happen. Some of them will be outside your control. Therefore, you need to have a robust crisis management program in place. You hope never to have to use it, but you want it to be there when you need it. Your call may come without warning. You need to be ready 24/7.

Thank you for working on crisis preparedness for your organization. Crisis management programs are a journey of constant improvement. You never will cross a finish line, because there isn't one. You will, however, get better every year, and when the big crisis comes, you will be ready. Having read this book and considered its suggestions, you are well on your way to having the knowledge and tools to be an effective Corporate Smokejumper—one who is well equipped when the alarm sounds.

Corporate Smokejumper

GLOSSARY

Accountability The quality of being open, straightforward and accessible and, when a crisis occurs, willingness to acknowledge appropriate responsibility.

Alert System The mechanisms by which a crisis team is notified of a need to activate. (See Section 9.1)

Anomaly An irregularity or an outlier. Something that deviates from the norm or the expected.

Box Your Thoughts Tool A technique for organizing the team's input, especially during the initial meeting for a crisis response. (See Section 10.4)

Core Team The central, hands-on group that does the work of managing the crisis. The Core Team should include one person from each key function, discipline, or group. (See Section 11.3)

Core Values Indisputable concepts—both real and bold—that guide an organization and can serve as a solid foundation from which to manage the continuity of a company's response to any crisis. When core values are cited over the course of the crisis, people will see a consistent theme and will recognize that even though a company may be struggling with the complexity of a situation, it is guided by higher principles.

Core Statement or Core Content A dynamic, not static, statement that describes the emerging situation, includes the company's position, and is updated as often as necessary. The statement should be used as the core for all other communications. Often a simple introductory paragraph and closing are used to tailor the communication to a specific audience. At other times, more detail must be added.

Crisis (formal) An unexpected company-related event of a nature and magnitude that meets all of the following conditions: adversely affects the normal operations, conduct of business, reputation, or financial position of the company; requires an immediate, coordinated management response; has the potential to quickly focus extensive media and public attention on the company.

Crisis (informal) A potentially high-profile situation where the organization is faced with a range of bad choices. An acute situation that requires high-stakes decisions despite too little information—or faulty information—and too little time before moving into the public spotlight where everyone will second-guess what you decide to do.

Crisis Drill A practice session intended to simulate the feel of a real crisis where the parts are actively moving, with people doing some of the things they actually would do during a real-life crisis. Phone calls are placed and answered; emails are sent; requests for information may go to people not directly working on the drill. The purpose of the drill, which is designed not only to be realistic but to push the limits of the team, is to find gaps in the Crisis Management Plan and to highlight areas for improvement. (See Section 8.3)

Crisis Management An organization's preparation for and response to a situation that meets its definition of a crisis.

Crisis Management Plan The master document that defines the operations of the Crisis Team from its structure and preparedness to the roles and responsibilities during response to a crisis. The plan can include appendices such as response guides, check lists and contact lists.

Crisis Team The standing committee of an organization that directs Crisis Management for a defined segment of the organization. Also, a designated group assigned the task of responding to a specific situation that has been deemed a crisis.

Critical Unknowns Important elements (facts, conditions) that lack clarity or complete understanding, especially at the outset of a crisis.

Debrief A process to aid in the capture and sharing of the lessons learned from a specific crisis response. Various organizations use different terms for similar processes, such as post mortem or after-action report. (See Section 17.1)

Decision Tree A framework that uses a tree-like graph or model of choices and their possible consequences.

Electronic Team Room A secure space, such as a SharePoint site, where crisis team members can store their plans, checklists and contact lists, share communications materials, track progress, and manage the many moving parts of a crisis.

Holistic Assessment An approach that takes in the many dimensions of a situation and results in a comprehensive plan that addresses all crucial aspects. For a successful long-term resolution to the crisis, the team must see the complete picture in order to understand the scope of the problem and find a solution for the entire situation, not just parts of it.

In-scope Situations Those problems that should be managed under your Crisis Management Plan.

Issue A gap between an organization's actions and the expectations of it stakeholders. An ongoing internal or external condition that must be met with an orderly response before it can have a significant adverse effect on the functioning and future interests of the organization, i.e., a protracted situation that must be managed before becoming a crisis.

Issue Management The long-term strategic approach to closing a gap between an organization's actions and the expectations of its stakeholders. Typically, Issue Management involves anticipating trends, responding to challenging events and engaging critical stakeholders on an ongoing basis.

Key Vulnerabilities Factors that may make an organization particularly susceptible to attack or harm. These factors may relate directly or indirectly to the crisis being managed.

Lead Time The amount of time available for preparation before a specific crisis strikes.

Martyr Syndrome The tendency for some crisis team members to unduly sacrifice to the point that their health, family life or quality of work suffer. (See Section 12.7)

Out-of-scope Situations Those problems that should not be managed under your Crisis Management Plan.

Pause & Reflect Tool A means for helping a crisis team assess the challenges that face them, especially in midstream. The Pause & Reflect Tool allows the team to analyze a thorny problem that has been resistant to all resolution efforts to date. Also, the tool can be used when conditions change substantially, as they sometimes do. At such times, the tool allows the team to step back to reassess exactly what problem they are trying to address. (See Section 14.4)

Process Leader The person who directs how the team will operate and who facilitates team meetings in an orderly and efficient manner. Ideally, the process manager is a crisis leader separate from any other leader already wearing a different hat on the team. (See Section 11.2)

Records Management Careful creation and retention of records related to a crisis situation. It's helpful to have a qualified attorney address this topic. Sooner or later, especially in the U.S., a crisis usually involves litigation. Any notes people take may need to be preserved. It is a good idea for the attorney to provide guidance at the outset on how information should be recorded and by whom. (See Section 10.3)

Redundancies Alternative means to accomplish every task for all crucial parts of the system.

Resources A ring of team members beyond the Core Team, to be viewed as expanded or "critical" resources who can provide support in workstreams or sub-groups. (See Section 11.4) Also, the equipment needed to effectively address the situation.

Response Guide A brief document, usually one page, that outlines the high priority initial tasks that must be completed and who is going to do them for a particular type of crisis. Response guides supplement the overall crisis plan and are created for high probability/high impact threats.

Situation Leader The person who is hands-on leading the Core Team, who makes the major decisions and who sees that they are efficiently and effectively carried out. This person updates senior-level sponsors on a regular basis. (See Section 11.1)

Situation Assessment A means of adding structure to the first crisis meeting to assist in calming people and getting an efficient process started. One person should describe the situation as it is known and understood at the outset of a developing crisis. Use of the Box Your Thoughts Tool (See Section 10.4) will engage the crisis team members in the assessment and organization of all important information to date with the knowledge that they will continue to clarify the understanding of the situation in the near future.

Smokejumpers Highly disciplined, well-trained firefighters who carry their tools, gear, and supplies with them when they parachute into remote areas to combat wildfires, hoping to reach a developing fire and extinguish it before it becomes a raging inferno.

Social Media The collection of social networks that compose a dynamic, interactive force all over the world. Social media are computer-mediated technologies that allow the creating and sharing of information, news, ideas, opinions and other forms of expression via virtual communities and networks. The social media allow individuals to communicate with each other and companies through multi-layered, multi-directional, instantaneous transmission of information.

Spokesperson The person who represents the company in interactions with stakeholders, most particularly the news media. (See Section 13.1)

Sponsors Designated upper-level managers of the company who oversee the operations of the Core Team. The sponsors are responsible for resources, policy decisions, and ensuring that the team understands the bigger picture regarding the impacts and outcomes of what they are deciding and doing.

Stakeholders The individuals or groups—internal and external— who likely will have an interest in the situation and its outcome. Examples: the community, government officials, shareholders, customers, employees.

Stewardship Anticipating and addressing the needs and expectations of key stakeholders in a responsible and timely manner.

Strategic Program A master plan for crisis management, often created at the beginning of each year, to address major work areas such as training, crisis team exercises, planning, systems and facilities, upgrades, and meetings. Together with a rolling five-year outlook, a strategic program helps to ensure that a company is moving its overall crisis management effort forward. This practice also creates an opportunity to review the program with your senior leaders and discuss any gaps or needs.

Supply Chain A system of organizations, people, activities, information, and resources involved in moving a product or service from supplier to customer. Crises can develop at almost any point along the chain.

Tabletop Exercise A scenario-based discussion among the members of one or more crisis teams. It provides an opportunity to explore how teams would function when dealing with a real-world situation, but without actually implementing the actions. A tabletop exercise is less elaborate and time consuming than a crisis drill. (See Section 8.3)

Time Drivers Time constraints such as product delivery deadlines, news media deadlines, regulatory requirements for reporting to the government, and other such factors that will determine when certain crisis response actions must be performed.

Traditional Media Print-based or traditional electronic news media such as radio and television that operate in a transmission model that is largely one-directional: from one content creator to many receivers. All of these formats have become somewhat interactive through their websites and blogs, but in general they lack the ability to engage instantaneously and cannot match the speed or the multi-directional reach of the social media networks.

Transparency The quality of openness, honesty, and accountability that exhibits the organization's intention to share information with the community, shareholders, employees, customers, or other stakeholders.

Vulnerability Assessment A formal survey designed to ask selected employees across a diagonal slice of the organization what current or future crisis threats concern them and how well prepared they believe the organization is. (See Section 7.2)

War Room A room in which a crisis team can meet during a crisis. (See Section 9.3)

Workstreams The areas of activity that feed into the overall project. For complex crisis situations, there will be multiple workstreams running on parallel tracks. The Core Team member for each functional area is accountable for staying on top of the tasks being done in that arena. There likely will be cross linkages among the workstreams, and the Process Leader must furnish a timetable to make sure they do not become entangled or inefficient. (See Section 11.5)

Acknowledgements

I am honored to have worked with many bright and talented people over the years. In ways large and small, I have learned from them. I am grateful to one and all, named and unnamed here.

Cathy Andriadis

Glen Baldwin

Tom Barry

Cathie Barton

Ray Beaudry

Dave Boothe

Jim Borel

Jane Brooks

Trudy Bryan

Lori Captain

Ann Cardinal

Courtney Chabot-Dreyer

Kate Childress

Michael Clarke

Tom Connelly

Paul Costello

Lew Crampton

Teresa Yancey Crane

Bill Currey

Rick Deadwyler

Silvio DeCarli

Lou Delvecchio

AnnaMaria DeSalva

Paul Dice

Markus Dietrich

Lisa Dry

Jeff Dunkel

Krish Dutta

Nick Everhart

Anthony Farina

Raymond Forney

Kathy Forte

Ray Germann

Paul Gilding

Frank Gilmore

Dan Goicoechea

Jennifer Goldston

Roger Goodman

Richard Goodmanson

Mike Hanretta

Paul Heck

Chad Holliday

Tony Hoppa

Tom Humphrey

Don Hunton

Greg Jeanes	Ed Montooth	Tom Sager
Don Johnson	Robert Moran	Peter Sandman
Xu Jun	Michael Mudd	Yale Schalk
Doyle Karr	Bob Nelson	Dave Schmidt
Tom Keefer	Jim O'Hare	Gregg Schmidt
Bill Kirk	Kathy O'Keefe	John Sieg
Kelli Kukura	Rick Olson	Craig Skaggs
Ellen Kullman	Joseph Oommen	Gerry Smith
Mini Lam	Kathy Palokoff	Janet Smith
Ricky Law	Nate Pepper	Gary Spitzer
Barry Lindley	Lissa Perlman	Tom Stenzel
Irv Lipp	Jim Pesek	Rick Straitman
Carl Lukach	Joan Platz	Dan Turner
Jack Malloy	Jim Porter	Tim Vaux
Terry Medley	Dave Quinn	Don Verrico
Eduardo Menchaca	Bill Raisch	Patti Walters
Gil Meyer Sr.	Heather Read	Clif Webb
Jeff Meyer	Kent Reasons	John Weber
Nick Meyer	Martha Rees	David Weir
Susan Meyer	Clyde Roberts	Tom West
Justin Miller	Jo Robertson	Bob Wilkerson
Rik Miller	Sylvia Rowe	Sylvia Williams
Stacey Mobley	Bill Ruckelshaus	

About
the Author

Gil Meyer is a crisis management expert, recognized and sought after speaker, and trainer. With decades of experience at the front lines of critical situations, Gil knows what it takes to manage and inspire creative change in crisis management.

Gil worked for DuPont for 29 years serving in a wide range of Public Affairs and Regulatory Affairs roles. For 12 years he directed the corporate global issues and crisis management programs for DuPont.

While leading the "all risks" crisis management program at this highly diversified company, Gil coordinated response to a wide range of situations including the Katrina/Rita hurricanes, the financial crisis, the H1N1 pandemic of 2009, the 2011 Japan earthquake, Superstorm Sandy, industrial accidents and a variety of product quality challenges.

Gil gives presentations and conducts workshops on crisis management, emerging issues, and future trends. For six years he served as chair of the Board of Directors of the Issue Management Council. Previously he held positions on the Board of Directors and Executive Committee of the International Food Information Council (IFIC), a leading organization of the food industry.

Gil and his wife live in the Potomac Highlands west of Washington, D.C. where they enjoy kayaking, mountain biking, and hiking. Gil holds a bachelor's degree in journalism and a master's degree in plant pathology, both from West Virginia University.

CPSIA information can be obtained
at www.ICGtesting.com
Printed in the USA
LVOW13s1537080317
526553LV00012B/1481/P